# EATING WATER, DRINKING SOUP

## FINDING NOURISHMENT IN THE DEEPEST PAIN

Dr. Paula Davis

Disclaimer This book is intended for educational and reflective purposes only. It does not constitute psychological, psychiatric, medical, or other professional advice, nor does it replace individual assessment, diagnosis, or treatment by a qualified professional. Although grounded in trauma-informed research and clinical experience, the material may evoke emotional responses in some readers. If you experience distress, please seek support from a suitably qualified professional.



Publication Details
ISBN: 978-0-6451179-1-2 eBook
ISBN: 978-0-6451179-5-0 Print

First published 2026 in Australia

# BOOKS BY THE SAME AUTHOR

*After the Breaking: Psychological Trauma and Collective Healing*

*Exploring the Roots of Heartache: The Stories Our Pain is Trying to Tell*

*A Safe Place: A Marriage Enrichment Resource Manual*

# PROFESSIONAL AND READER CARE NOTICE

This book is a work of psychological realism. While it draws on established trauma theory, attachment research, and the author's clinical and educational experience, it is written for educational and reflective purposes. It is not intended to provide psychological, psychiatric, medical, or therapeutic treatment, nor to replace individual assessment or care from a qualified professional.

Some material may resonate deeply or evoke personal memories, emotional responses, or unresolved trauma. Such responses are not uncommon when engaging with trauma-informed content. Readers are encouraged to attend gently to their own limits and to seek appropriate professional support if distress becomes overwhelming or persistent.

The aim of this book is understanding, reflection, and growth, not diagnosis or treatment. Healing from trauma is relational and often requires personalised care within a safe therapeutic context.

*To my granddaughters, with love and wisdom, so that you may carry a piece of my heart with you wherever you go.*

*To my children, Mark and Rebecca and their partners, the dreamers who refuse to let the world define them.*

*To my husband Barry, who taught me the value of storytelling and was there with me through every word and every page.*

*"If the water kills you, what can you do to the water? You make soup with the water and eat it." ~ East African Workshop Participant on Grief*

*"Nothing is ever too far gone for hope to come find you." ~ Unknown*

# CONTENTS

# LIST OF TABLES

# LIST OF FIGURES

# FOREWORD

In recent decades, neuroscience has illuminated incredible truths about the human brain - perhaps none more remarkable than its plasticity. We now understand that the brain is not fixed or static; it adapts, rewires, and regenerates, even in the face of deep trauma. This knowledge has ushered in a wave of research and literature exploring Post-Traumatic Stress Disorder (PTSD), with many approaches focusing on rewiring thought patterns, calming hyperactive nervous systems, and offering coping mechanisms rooted in cognitive science.

And yet, as vast and varied as this literature is, it often overlooks a foundational truth: we are not just brains and bodies, but souls - eternal beings made in the image of God. A purely clinical or cognitive approach, while valuable, is incomplete. It speaks to the symptoms but often misses the soul.

What our friend Paula offers in this book is deeply needed and refreshingly rare - a holistic path to healing that centres Christ and embraces the whole person. Rooted in empathy, naked bravery, and the transforming love of Jesus, this work dares to face trauma not as something to be erased, but as something that can be redeemed. Here, even the most painful experiences are stirred into something nourishing - like a healing soup, rich with meaning and grace.

This book is more than a collection of insights or stories. It is a sanctuary. A place where brokenness meets grace. Where theological depth and lived experience are held in holy tension. Paula has written with raw honesty and breathtaking vulnerability -

not as one who stands above pain, but as one who has walked through it, hand in hand with the Healer.

Each chapter is a balm for the soul and a call to courage. Whether you are navigating deep sorrow, hidden shame, spiritual disillusionment, or the silent ache of unanswered questions, this book will meet you there - not with easy answers, but with sacred companionship.

Through Scripture, insight, and a heartfelt journey, this book offers a way to reconcile with shame, to see wounds not as permanent scars but as places where healing light can shine through. It doesn't just offer tools for coping, but an invitation to feel loved, being reinvented, and transformed - whole and free in Christ.

We pray that as you read, you will feel the gentle pursuit of the One who weeps with you, heals you, and calls you by name. And like Paula, may you too find nourishment in the places you never thought you could survive.

With love and gratitude.

Drs. Sam & Sanaa Labib, General Practitioners

# INTRODUCTION

*"Nothing is ever too far gone for hope to come find you." —Unknown*

## The Pursuit Of Healing

Have you ever felt too broken to be loved? Too wounded to be healed? Too exhausted to keep trying?

I have, and perhaps you have too.

There's an old poem I've returned to many times: "The Hound of Heaven" by Francis Thompson. In it, the poet describes a soul fleeing from God, not out of rebellion but out of pain, convinced they are too broken to be loved. Yet God pursues them with "unhurrying chase and unperturbed pace," not to punish, but to heal.

That image speaks to something I've lived repeatedly: the quiet, persistent way God follows us through our shame, exhaustion, numbness, and fear. He comes not in fury, but in mercy, not to expose our weakness, but to meet us in it.

This book was born in one of those seasons of flight and pursuit.

## When Trauma Finds Us Again

I had just returned from working in a country ravaged by decades of war. The people I met there had lost everything, homes, loved ones, entire ways of life. Yet they welcomed me with such grace and generosity that I felt like I was the one being healed. My role was to help them, but often I found myself the student.

Coming home, I expected to rest. I wanted to collapse into the comfort of routine, of familiar faces, of quiet. But peace did not come. Instead, I was blindsided.

A deeply personal accusation, deeply wounding, was hurled at me by someone I loved. I didn't see it coming. I couldn't explain myself in a way they could hear. I felt emotionally ambushed, my heart folding in on itself. I went silent, not out of choice but out of pain. I shut down.

Only later did I recognize it as a trauma response. When the body perceives threat, not always physical, but emotional, it instinctively protects itself. I'd worked with countless clients on this. I knew it clinically. But knowing it and living it are two different things.

Then came Christmas. A time meant for celebration, connection, joy. Instead, it brought conflict. Another rupture. Words that wounded. Reactions that stung. And me, sitting on the veranda, while laughter drifted out from the living room, crying like a child whose world had just broken open. I didn't want to feel. I wanted to disappear.

These experiences, which we'll revisit throughout this book, left me reeling. I didn't expect to be so triggered. I didn't expect the sorrow to run so deep. I found myself asking questions that perhaps you've asked too:

> *Will there ever be an end to this pain?*
> *Can I heal from these repeated wounds, or am I doomed to circle them forever?*
> *How do I find my way back to joy when everything inside of me feels crushed?*
> *How do I help others heal when I myself am drowning in sorrow?*

What do we do with these moments? The ones that awaken not just our current pain but every buried ache we've learned to ignore. How do we stay present when all we want is to run?

It felt like I was being undone from the inside out. But over time, I've come to see it differently. I wasn't falling apart; I was being found.

## For Anyone Who Has Ever Felt Shattered

This book is for you, the one sitting in church with a smile that doesn't reach your eyes. The professional who's built a competent life but can't silence the voice that says you're not enough. The parent, pastor, counsellor, or friend who carries others while wondering if your own story matters.

It's for anyone who has known trauma, whether dramatic or quiet, recognized or hidden.
Because trauma locks us into old stories. It replays familiar lies: *You're too much. You're not enough. You'll never be safe.* But these are not God's words.

In the chapters ahead, we'll journey together through some of the deepest valleys of my life and the lives of those I've walked beside. We'll explore what trauma does to our identity, our relationships, and our view of God, and how healing becomes possible when truth, grace, and presence collide.

That's what "The Hound of Heaven" reminds me: we don't always recognize God's pursuit as love. Sometimes it feels like disruption, like exposure. But it is always love. The kind that won't let us numb ourselves forever. The kind that sits beside us in our exhaustion and gently whispers, "Let's look at this together."

## Why "Eating Water, Drinking Soup"?

The title of this book comes from a phrase I once heard used to describe absurd endurance. It evokes a time when everything is upside down, when what should nourish us doesn't, when comfort slips through our fingers. In trauma, life can feel exactly like that, inside out, senseless, surreal. And strangely, these are often the very places where healing begins.

As we'll discover in Chapter 1, time alone doesn't heal our deepest wounds. But God does, not by bypassing our pain, but by entering it with us.

## Three Strands Woven Together

This book brings together three strands of my life:

1. **Clinical insight**, drawn from over three decades of working in trauma recovery, both in Australia and in post-conflict regions.
2. **Personal story**, offered with honesty and vulnerability, not as someone who has arrived, but as a fellow traveller in the healing journey.
3. **Spiritual reflection**, rooted in Scripture and the relentless love of a God who pursues our hearts and restores our souls.

These strands don't sit in neat compartments. They're woven together. You'll find professional wisdom entwined with the raw ache of my own healing, and spiritual insights rising from places I didn't choose to go, but where grace met me anyway.

## Your Journey Through This Book

The book is divided into four parts, each building on the previous:

**Part 1: Wounds and the God Who Heals** We begin by confronting the myth that time heals all wounds, as you'll see in the first chapter. Deep psychological, emotional, and spiritual pain lingers unless we address it intentionally. Here, we meet God not just as a distant observer, but as the healer of heart, mind, and soul.

**Part 2: The War Within: Shame and Identity** This section explores the hidden battle between shame and truth; how distorted beliefs and wounded identity shape our lives. We begin to unearth the lies we've agreed to and trace the path back toward freedom.

**Part 3: Exploring the Roots of Heartache** We dig into the strongholds of shame, anxiety, chronic stress, and depression. These are not just emotional states; they are responses to pain. Here, we discover how honesty, surrender, and truth can reshape our inner world.

**Part 4: Breaking Free: From Strangleholds to Strength** This final section focuses on breaking free from the inner strongholds that keep us bound. Repentance, renewed thinking, and deeper intimacy with God lead us from fear into freedom.
By the time we reach the end, my hope is that you'll not only understand trauma differently, but that you'll have practical, spiritual pathways toward the healing your heart longs for.

## Companions For Your Journey

At the end of each chapter, you'll find simple practices designed to move these truths from your head to your heart:

- **Declarations** to speak life over your heart and relationships.
- **A Guided Prayer** to open space for God's presence and healing.
- **Reflection Questions** to invite deeper personal or shared exploration.
- **A Journal Prompt** to engage with the chapter's themes.

These aren't tasks or checklists, but gentle invitations, ways to linger, listen, and respond to what stirs in you. Take what you need. Let the rest wait. There is no rush here.

As we progress through the book, these practices will build upon each other, creating a pathway from understanding to transformation.

## When Faith Is Real, But The Pain Is Too

As a trauma counsellor, I understand how trauma distorts our thinking, numbs our emotions, and fragments our sense of self. But as a follower of Jesus, I believe that God does not bypass our humanity to heal us; He enters it. He meets us in the wound.

Frederick Buechner once said, "Listen to your life, because if God speaks to us at all, it is into our personal lives that He speaks." That's what I've learned to do: to listen. Not just to the tidy parts of my life, but to the messy, hurting, unfinished parts. The places where God has tracked me down like the Hound of Heaven, not to reprimand, but to remind me: *You are seen. You are loved. You are mine.*

So, if you find yourself weary, or wondering where God has gone, or struggling to believe that healing could still be possible, know this: You are not too far gone. And God is not done pursuing you.

Even when we're eating water and drinking soup. Even when joy feels like a distant memory.

Even then, grace finds us.

Hope comes quietly. And healing begins...

# PART 1

*Wounds and the God Who Heals*

# CHAPTER 1

## *Time Does Not Heal All Wounds*

---

*"Lord my God, I called to you for help, and you healed me." ~ Psalm 30:2*

*"Heal me Lord, and I will be healed..." ~ Jeremiah 17:14*

*"The most profound thing we have to offer our own children is our own healing." ~ Anne Lamott*

---

### The Myth Of Time As Healer

We've all heard it said: "Time heals all wounds." It's what we tell the grieving widow, the betrayed spouse, the traumatized child. *Just wait. It will get better. You'll move on.*

But what if this well-meaning advice is fundamentally flawed?

What if time alone doesn't heal, but merely distances us from our pain, covering wounds without cleaning them?

### From Transaction To Transformation

I was twenty-one, newly married, and searching for purpose and meaning. At a packed seminar on inner healing and deliverance, my husband and I sat desperate to be filled with the Holy Spirit. The teachings promised freedom from emotional wounds, trauma, and relational pain.

We followed every formula meticulously. Confess this sin. Pray these words. Claim this scripture. Renounce that influence.

It felt like God was a cosmic slot machine: insert the right behaviour, say the right words, and healing, blessings, and peace would come tumbling out. But what we got wasn't a relationship; it was a transaction. And we were left feeling disillusioned.

This experience, one of many I'll share throughout this book, marked the beginning of my understanding that true healing isn't about formulas or quick fixes.

Time passed. We followed Jesus faithfully, attended church, served in ministry. But my woundedness lingered. Deep down, I began to wonder: Why hadn't God healed me? Was I doing something wrong? Did I not have enough faith?

I used to believe that time healed all wounds. But now I know the truth: **Time alone doesn't heal.** Just as a deep physical injury needs cleaning, stitching, and careful tending, so do the wounds of the heart, mind, body, and spirit. Healing requires presence, not just passage of days.

## Avoiding The Shortcuts

Theologian Robert Mulholland (2006) describes healing as a grace-filled transformation into the image of Christ. But too often, Christians are taught to bypass the pain:

- "Just forgive and move on"
- "Give it to God"
- "Don't dwell on the past"
- "Count your blessings instead"

These well-meaning phrases can unintentionally shut down the process of true healing. They offer an escape from discomfort, not an invitation to transformation. They reflect our cultural aversion to pain, even the necessary pain of growth.

The Bible speaks of four aspects of the self: mind, body, emotions, and spirit. Trauma can splinter each of these, leaving us disoriented and disconnected, even from God. Recovery, then, must address all four dimensions of our being. We need more than prayer, more than time, more than distraction, we need God's presence within a safe space to grieve, question, and be restored.

## The Pike In The Tank: When We Stop Hoping

Years ago, I came across a story that pierced my heart. Researchers placed a large northern pike into a glass tank with its favourite food, small minnows. Initially, it feasted easily. Then they inserted a sheet of glass between the pike and the minnows.

The pike continued to lunge at its prey but slammed into the invisible barrier. Again and again, it tried, only to be stopped by pain. Eventually, the pike gave up.
When the researchers removed the glass divider, something remarkable happened, or rather, didn't happen. The minnows swam freely around the tank. But the pike no longer pursued them. It had learned that hope only brought pain.

I was moved when I first heard this story. Not just intellectually, but viscerally. Because *I had become the pike.*

Repeated blows to my spirit had trained me to stop trying. Somewhere deep inside, I believed nothing would change. My wounds would remain forever raw. Healing was for other people, not me.

The enemy of our souls loves this strategy: If he can't destroy us, he'll convince us to settle. He'll whisper:

> "Don't risk it."
> "Don't believe again."
> "Stay where it's safe."

But Jesus doesn't leave us in the glass tank. He comes to restore what was lost.
In John 10:10, Jesus declares: "The thief comes only to steal and kill and destroy. I have come that they may have life and have it to the full." This promise isn't just about eternal life, it's about abundant life now, even in the midst of our wounds.

Healing takes courage. It often begins not with a dramatic breakthrough, but with a whisper of hope:

- When we dare to believe again after disappointment.
- When we allow ourselves to grieve what was lost.
- When we stop pretending that we're fine and bring our honest pain into God's presence.

God is not afraid of our wounds. He meets us there, not to shame or scold, but to gently lead us into life.

## A Longing For Healing And Wholeness

"Time is a great healer," we tell each other to provide comfort. But this well-meaning sentiment often fails to acknowledge a crucial truth: while physical wounds are visible and their healing progress can be tracked, wounds to the mind, soul, heart, and spirit remain hidden, sometimes even from ourselves.

For years, I couldn't connect my anxiety, depression, and chronic anger to frozen, painful life-wounds that had never been properly addressed. These unhealed injuries silently shaped my responses, relationships, and resilience. Like water finding the path of least resistance, my emotional reactions flowed through channels carved by old pain.

Life-wounds block abundance. They limit our capacity to receive love, to trust, to hope. I longed for healing from past wounds that were still alive in the present. But a question nagged at me: *Does God care about these inner injuries as much as our physical ones?*

## God's Heart For Our Healing

The Bible contains many verses about healing. Here are just a few that have sustained me:

- "I am the Lord who heals you" (Exodus 15:26).
- "But I will restore you to health and heal your wounds,' declares the Lord..." (Jeremiah 30:17).
- "As a mother comforts her child, so I will comfort you..." (Isaiah 66:13).
- "Jesus graciously welcomed them and talked to them about the kingdom of God. Those who needed healing, he healed" (Luke 9:10-11).
- "Lord, you know how I long for my health once more. You hear my every sigh" (Psalm 38:9).
- "Yes, I will bless the Lord and not forget the glorious things he does for me. He forgives all my sins. He heals me" (Psalm 103:2-3).

As I explored these passages, I discovered that humans are multi-dimensional beings. Wholeness and healing require a multi-faceted approach.

Matthew 4:23-25 says, "From there he went all over Galilee... He also healed people of their diseases and of the bad effects of their bad lives... People brought anybody with a sickness, whether mental, emotional, or physical. Jesus healed them, one and all."

He healed complex beings like me, not just bodies, but souls, minds, and spirits too.
Mark 12:29-31 gives another clue about this complexity: "'Love the Lord your God with all your heart and with all your soul and with all your mind and with all your strength.' The second is this: 'Love your neighbour as yourself.' There is no commandment greater than these."

This perspective illuminates that healing isn't just about physical restoration. It's about addressing the heart, soul, mind, and strength, the entirety of who we are. True healing invites us to love God, love others, and love ourselves with the fullness of our being. In that space of divine love, we find hope for wholeness and restoration.

## Closing Thoughts

We are often told that time heals all wounds. But anyone who has lived through profound loss, betrayal, or trauma knows this isn't always true.

Time may mute the sharp edges of pain, but it does not resolve what has been buried. Unattended wounds settle into the soul, shaping our beliefs, behaviours, and sense of self. They become silent narratives influencing how we view our worth, whom we trust, even how we perceive God.

True healing asks more of us than simply waiting. It invites us to turn toward our pain, to listen, and to feel what we've long avoided. Healing requires presence. Compassion. And courage.

Often, the first movement toward healing comes through tears. Not the polite tears we brush away quickly, but the deep, unbidden ones, the tears that surprise us, expose us, and sometimes undo us. These are the tears of the heart, rising from places words cannot reach.

They signal that something hidden is stirring, aching to be seen. Though we may fear them, such tears are not a sign of weakness, they are sacred. They soften the soul's protective shell and become a gateway to tenderness, connection, and restoration.

In the chapters ahead, we'll explore how trauma affects not just our emotions but our entire being. We'll uncover how unhealed wounds shape our thoughts, choices, and relationships. And most importantly, we'll discover pathways to the healing God longs to bring, not because we've performed the right religious transaction, but because His very nature is to restore.

In the breaking open, something begins to shift. And that's where we're headed next.

---

## Declarations

I declare that my wounds do not define me; God is restoring every part of me: heart, soul, mind, and strength.

I declare that I will hope again; God is with me in my pain, and He is making all things new.

I declare that I am not alone; God walks with me through every valley, and His presence is my healing.

I declare that I receive God's grace today; His love empowers me to love Him, love others, and love myself.

---

## Prayer

*Father in Heaven,*
*You see every part of me, my story, my scars, my longings, and my fears. Thank You that I am not beyond Your reach. You do not rush my healing, but You gently lead me toward wholeness. I bring You the parts of me that feel too broken, too tired, too afraid. Come, Holy Spirit, breathe life into what has felt numb, and light into what has been hidden. Restore what was stolen. Mend what was shattered. Teach me to love You with all of who I am, heart, soul, mind, and strength. I choose to trust Your presence even when I don't understand Your timing. Let Your love be the ground I stand on, the truth I live by, and the grace that carries me forward. In Jesus' name, amen!*

## Reflection Questions

1. How have past wounds contributed to who I am today?
2. What indicators suggest that I am effectively healing or not healing from past emotional wounds?
3. What unhealthy coping mechanisms am I currently employing?
4. How effective are my current coping strategies?
5. To what extent do I genuinely believe in my current capacity for loving God with all my heart, soul, mind, and strength?

## Journal Prompt

Write or draw a short prayer or reflection: What do I sense God whispering to my heart today? Let your pen move without censoring. See what flows out.

# CHAPTER 2

## *Tears That Open the Heart*

---

*"You keep track of all my sorrows.*
*You have collected all my tears in your bottle.*
*You have recorded each one in your book." ~ Psalm 56:8 (NLT)*

*"Jesus wept." ~ John 11:35*

*"The Christian life is not a constant high. I have my moments of deep discouragement. I have to go to God in prayer with tears in my eyes, and say, 'O God, forgive me,' or 'Help me.'" ~ Billy Graham, Grace Life International*

---

### When Tears Become Teachers

I didn't always trust tears. For a long time, I saw them as something to manage, or better yet, hide. They made me feel exposed, out of control, and somehow... weak. Especially in a world that often praises strength, composure, and "getting on with things." But over time, I've come to see that tears can be holy. Not something to suppress, but something to listen to.

Because when tears finally come, those unexpected, soul-deep ones, they often carry truths we haven't dared to speak. They rise from places we've buried and long forgotten. And in their tender flow, something begins to shift. Hardened ground softens. Defences falter. The heart begins to open.

This chapter is about those moments. The ones when pain finally breaks through the surface, not to destroy us, but to invite us toward healing. Toward honesty. Toward God.

Let me invite you into a reflection on my husband's tears...

## Reflections From Evans Head

For much of my adult life, I didn't cry. It wasn't that I didn't want to, it's just that I couldn't. Somewhere along the way, I had learned to shut down emotions. Tears were seen as weakness, and weakness felt unsafe. I had become emotionally disconnected from myself, from God, and from others.

The turning point came years later, in a quiet moment with God. I don't remember what triggered it, but I suddenly began to weep, deep, wrenching sobs that came from a place I hadn't touched in years. It was as if a dam broke. And with it came healing.

Tears, I've come to believe, are not signs of failure. They're signs of life.
I had spent so long protecting myself from pain that I also shut myself off from joy, connection, and love. I had become like that pike in the glass tank. Somewhere deep inside, I believed there was no safe place for my vulnerability. So, I learned to stay behind the glass.

But God is our safe place.

He doesn't demand performance or perfection. He simply asks us to come. To let the defences fall. To bring our sorrow, shame, and longing to Him. In the Psalms, David writes, *"You have collected all my tears in your bottle. You have recorded each one in your book"* (Psalm 56:8). God sees. God knows. God remembers.

When I allowed myself to weep, I found Jesus weeping with me. Not rushing me to move on but staying present with my pain. His tenderness undid me. And it began to restore what had been lost.

Our world doesn't often give men permission to cry. But Jesus does. He invites us into wholeness, not by demanding strength, but by welcoming weakness. I'm still learning. But I've discovered that tears are a gift. They water the dry places of the soul. They soften what has grown hard. They create space for new life to grow.

And in those tears, I have found Him.

## A Quiet Moment Of Reflection

The year begins, and Paula and I find ourselves in one of our favourite spots at Evans Head. The world is still, and the day's quiet serenity provides a perfect backdrop for reflection. As the first cups of tea warm our hands and hearts, Paula reads selected excerpts from the feedback, "grabs," as we call them, from the participants in our Trauma Recovery Program. Their words resonate deeply with me, drawing me into their experiences. As I watch the steam rise from my tea, I find myself suspended between the memories of their stories and the peace of the moment.

## The Healing Power Of Vulnerability

Communication has always fascinated me, especially the way meaning takes shape in the listener's mind. I often wonder: what does my listener actually hear? The reflection diaries from our Trauma Recovery Program offer deep insights into this delicate exchange. Yet, one particular entry pulls me out of my reflective state.

This entry is different. It carries a raw honesty, a vulnerability that immediately draws me in. The young woman writes about an experience in the Tree of Life exercise, where participants were invited to connect with their pain in ways that bypassed logic and went straight to the heart. She speaks of her struggle with tears, tears that she feels she is not strong enough to shed. Her words echo in my mind, revealing the courage it takes to approach our deepest emotions, even when we fear what they might bring.

## The Power Of The Tree Of Life Exercise

In the Tree of Life exercise, we help participants dismantle the protective walls they've built, allowing them to engage with their pain in a way that transcends logic. This young woman's words take me back to that moment. I remember the stillness in the room as everyone faced their pain head-on. For her, this moment was marked by a fear of tears, a fear of what might happen if she let go. *"I am not strong enough to cry,"* she writes, her words trembling with vulnerability.

This powerful disclosure brings me face-to-face with my own assumptions. I've often viewed tears as a weakness, an idea I learned growing up in a home where crying was discouraged. My father, a Second World War veteran, never cried. Tears, to him, were a sign of weakness. Yet, as I sit with this young woman's words, I realize that her struggle with tears is not about weakness, it is an invitation to confront pain and find healing.

## Tears: A Sign Of Strength, Not Weakness

Her words challenge a deeply ingrained belief I've carried for years. Tears have always been a source of discomfort for me. Growing up in a family where vulnerability was suppressed, I've often felt that crying was something to hide, something that revealed my lack of strength. Yet, as I read her reflection, I begin to see tears for what they truly are: a release, a surrender, and often, the beginning of transformation. This young woman's courage to face her fear of tears shifts my perspective. I now understand that tears are not a sign of weakness but a profound expression of strength, a willingness to face pain and begin the journey of healing.

## A Conversation That Opens New Doors

Later that morning, Paula and I engage in a conversation that opens new doors in our relationship. We've been wrestling with the patterns that emerge when we're under pressure, especially after workshops. I confess that I've been struggling to feel connected, sensing a withdrawal from Paula. But as we talk, I begin to see that my own pattern is also at play. I tend to disconnect when Paula is struggling with something, like a migraine or stress. I've learned to retreat into myself, armour up, and manage the situation, but I realize now that this response is rooted in an old wound.

## Exploring Trauma Responses In Relationship

Our conversation takes an unexpected turn as Paula shares insights from a book she's reading, *Trauma* by Professor Gordon Turnbull (2012). We begin to trace the trauma responses that emerge in both of us. For me, disconnection is a way of protecting myself from the fear of being left alone with my pain. For Paula, it's a way of coping with her own emotional responses. We realize that both of us have been retreating into self-protection, unable to offer each other the safety we long for.

## Finding Safety In God And Each Other

This realization is both painful and eye-opening. Neither of us can be the safe place for the other when we need it most. Yet, I find comfort in my Heavenly Father, my true place of safety. In moments like this, I'm reminded that ministry and life are underpinned by inner strength (Ephesians 3:16), and when I neglect to replenish that strength, the consequences are real. I see that what's happening between Paula and me mirrors the struggles of the people we serve. We've been given an invitation to explore our own trauma responses and struggles, finding healing in the brokenness.

## The Paradox Of Healing

In these moments of tension and struggle, I'm reminded of the paradoxes that often define our healing journeys. I think of Jesus, who uses paradox to invite us into deeper wisdom. He tells us that unless a grain of wheat falls to the ground and dies, it cannot bear fruit. True life is found not in holding on but in letting go. In the same way, I'm learning that healing often comes not through avoidance but through engaging with our pain, allowing it to transform us. The journey is messy, uncertain, and full of paradox, but it is also where growth and transformation begin.

## Closing Thoughts

As we reflect on the themes of vulnerability, healing, and connection, it becomes clear that true transformation often emerges from the places we are most reluctant to go, our pain, our brokenness, and our fear. Tears, once seen as weakness, have proven to be a powerful doorway to deeper healing and intimacy, not only with God but with each other. In the quiet, raw moments where we allow ourselves to be vulnerable, God meets us, not with condemnation, but with the tender embrace of love and restoration.

Our journey is not about avoiding pain or striving for perfection, but about embracing the paradoxes of life: that in our brokenness, we find wholeness; in our vulnerability, we find strength; and in our tears, we find healing. It is through letting go that we begin to truly hold on to what is life-giving.

As I continue to learn, I'm reminded that healing is a process, one that doesn't always follow a neat path. It can feel messy, uncertain, and at times, deeply uncomfortable. But even in those moments of discomfort, God is present, guiding us toward wholeness and offering us His peace. We are not called to perform or to hold it all together. We are called to come, just as we are, broken and beautiful, ready to be restored.

So, as we move forward in this journey together, let us remember that God is our safe place. He does not ask us to hide our pain or mask our vulnerability. Instead, He invites us to bring our whole selves, tears and all, into His presence, knowing that in doing so, we are being transformed from the inside out.

Healing is not the absence of pain, but the invitation to face it with courage, faith, and the assurance that we are never alone in the process. And in the end, it is in our willingness to embrace vulnerability, to sit with our pain, and to trust God's healing touch that we truly experience the fullness of life.

And perhaps this is where the greatest invitation lies: in learning to love, not in spite of our wounds, but through them. Because love, real love, is born in the crucible of vulnerability. It's easy to love when life is smooth, and our hearts are unscathed. But to love after betrayal, to open our hearts after they've been broken, to trust again after being let down, that is a different kind of courage. That is sacred ground.

As we step into the next chapter, we'll explore what it means to love God, ourselves, and others when our capacity to love has been shaped, and sometimes distorted, by the wounds we carry. How do we love when fear, shame, or self-protection rise up? How do we respond to Jesus' call to love with all our heart, soul, mind, and strength when parts of us feel numb, guarded, or fragmented?

This next chapter invites us deeper into the heart of transformation. Because love, the most important thing, is not just a feeling or a commandment. It is a journey of healing. It is the path by which we are restored.

---

## Declarations

I declare that vulnerability is not a weakness but a source of strength, for in my willingness to face my pain, I open the door to healing and transformation.

I declare that I am worthy of God's love and acceptance, and I choose to bring my whole self, brokenness and all, into His presence, trusting that He will restore and renew me.

I declare that healing is a process, and I will embrace the messy, uncomfortable moments with faith, knowing that God is present with me every step of the way.

I declare that tears are not a sign of failure but a profound expression of life, a release of what has been held too long, and a pathway to deeper intimacy with God and others.

---

## Prayer

*Father God,*
*Thank You for being my safe place, my refuge. I come before You today, bringing all that I am, my brokenness, my fears, and my pain. I ask for Your healing touch upon my heart, that I may have the courage to be vulnerable with You and with others.*
*Help me to see my tears not as weakness but as a sign of life, a release of what has been hidden too long. Teach me to trust You in the messy, uncomfortable spaces, knowing that You are always with me, guid-*

*ing me towards healing.*

*Thank You for Your grace and compassion, for not rushing me but staying with me in my sorrow. May I continue to grow in Your love and find strength in my surrender to You. In Jesus' name, Amen.*

---

## Reflection Questions

1. How have I viewed vulnerability in my own life? Do I see it as a weakness or a pathway to healing?
2. In what ways can I create space to confront and release the pain I've been holding onto?
3. What is one area where I feel disconnected, and how can I begin to reconnect with God or others in that space?
4. How have I seen God's presence in my struggles, and how has He been my safe place?
5. When have I experienced a moment of transformation, and how did embracing my pain lead to healing?

---

## Journal Prompt

Write or draw a short prayer or reflection: What part of my pain or vulnerability is God inviting me to bring into His healing presence today? Let your pen move without censoring. See what flows out.

# CHAPTER 3

## *Wounded Love*

---

*"When your heart is broken, you plant seeds in the cracks, and you pray for rain." ~ Andrea Gibson*

*"Tis better to have loved and lost than never to have loved at all." ~ Alfred Lord Tennyson*

*"My heart no longer felt as if it belonged to me. It now felt as if it had been stolen, torn from my chest by someone who wanted no part of it." ~ Meredith Taylor, Churning Water*

---

### The Most Important Thing: Loving God With All Of Me

The most important thing in life begins with loving God with all of me. Jesus put this commandment above all the rest: to love the Lord with all of our heart, soul, mind, and strength (Mark 12:30). It's not just a simple suggestion, it's foundational. In fact, if we don't obey this first commandment, we can't truly obey the others. Loving God is the heartbeat of everything that follows in the Bible.

Why does Jesus start here? Perhaps because loving God with our whole being is the key to everything that comes next. It's the only way to truly love others, to live in freedom, and to experience the full life that God offers. The commandment itself isn't complicated, but living it out, really living it, can feel overwhelming. It calls for more than just the occasional prayer or act of worship. It requires our whole self, our passions, prayers, intelligence, and energy. It requires that we love God not just with our emotions but with everything that we are, and everything that we have.

But what happens when our capacity to love is fractured? When betrayal, abandonment, or deep wounding makes it feel risky, even impossible, to love God or others wholeheartedly? This chapter explores what it means to love when you've been wounded, and how the first step to healing is taken not by striving harder, but by letting God's love reach the hidden, hurting places within us.

## The Nature Of Our Being: Heart, Soul, Mind, And Strength

I am not a theologian, and I don't pretend to be, but I do find myself fascinated by how Scripture speaks of us as being more than just bodies. We are spirit, soul, and body (1 Thessalonians 5:23). Jesus invites us to love God with our heart, soul, mind, and strength.

And these are not just metaphorical concepts; they represent different parts of our being. The heart (Greek *kardia*) represents the centre of our life, where beliefs, emotions, and thoughts all converge. The soul (*psyche*) speaks to our will and emotions, the mind (*dianoia*) refers to our thoughts and logic, and strength (*ischys*) encompasses our physical power, energy, and abilities (Bible Hub, n.d.). We are complex beings, and to love God with all of ourselves means acknowledging and engaging with every aspect of our humanity.

## The Interconnectedness Of Body, Soul, Mind, And Spirit

Bodily wounds are often more visible than the hidden pain within, yet both require attention. Physical injuries can lead to infection, disability, or even death if left untreated. Similarly, the soul, mind, and spirit are intricately connected to the body's functioning. The Apostle Paul's distinction between the physical and spiritual body highlights the holistic nature of humanity. While the physical body is tangible and visible, the spiritual body, our soul, mind, and spirit, profoundly shapes how we experience life, health, and healing. This interconnectedness means that emotional and spiritual healing can contribute to physical healing, and vice versa.

In Romans 12:1, Paul urges believers to present their bodies as living sacrifices, calling us to a holistic approach to life that honours God with our entire being, body, soul, mind, and spirit. By living in alignment with God's will, we can cultivate a state of well-being that encompasses every aspect of our being. Similarly, emotional and spiritual wounds can affect our physical health, just as physical wounds can carry spiritual or emotional consequences.

In essence, our body, soul, mind, and spirit are deeply interconnected, and healing in one area can lead to healing in others. This holistic process reflects God's desire for us to be whole.

## Loving God With Everything We Have

In the Old Testament, the soul represents the entirety of who we are, not just our emotions or our desires. When God created humanity, He formed us from the dust and breathed life into us, making us living souls (Genesis 2:7). This deep, all-encompassing love He calls us to isn't just for one area of our lives, it's meant to touch every part. It's meant to overflow into our families, our possessions, our work, our relationships, and even our digital lives. God wants us to love Him with everything we are and everything we have.

This truth is repeated throughout Scripture: God desires a love that flows from the core of who we are, a love that's authentic, sacrificial, and fully surrendered. It's not enough to love God with our hearts alone; our strength, minds, and very lives must also reflect this love.

## The Struggle To Love

And yet, I confess, I often feel overwhelmed by this command. It seems impossible to love God with everything I have when my capacity for love is so broken. From the very beginning, my ability to love, truly love, has been marred by wounds. I struggle to let love in, and I often fail to love others as I should. I know I'm not alone in this. It seems that we all bear the scars of a broken world.

Perhaps that's why Jesus' command feels so difficult. Love has been distorted for me by hurt, betrayal, and loss. But Jesus doesn't leave us in our brokenness. He offers us the gift of spiritual transformation. He invites us to bring our brokenness to Him so that He can heal us and restore our capacity to love.

## The Second Most Important Thing: Loving Others

The second most important thing, according to Jesus, is to *"love your neighbor as yourself"* (Mark 12:31). In many ways, this feels just as difficult, if not more so, than loving God. It's easy to talk about loving others, but when we struggle to love ourselves, how can we love others well? How can we offer something we haven't yet received?

I believe the key lies in understanding that we are loved first. As 1 John 4:19 (MSG) reminds us, *"First, we were loved, now we love. He loved us first."* Our capacity to love others is rooted in the deep, unconditional love of God that has already been poured out on us. When we grasp how deeply we are loved by our Creator, it empowers us to love others with the same grace and kindness.

## The Power Of Early Memories

Our earliest memories often shape the way we relate to God, to others, and even to ourselves. I remember one of my earliest experiences from kindergarten. We were supposed to bring a handkerchief to school each day. One day, I forgot mine. I was devastated. I began crying and couldn't stop, even though it seemed like such a small thing. It felt like the weight of the world had come crashing down on me.

Looking back, I realize that this small moment was one of the first experiences that shaped my sense of self-worth. I internalized shame from an early age, believing that if I didn't measure up or meet expectations, I wasn't lovable or worthy of care.

## Shame Is A Bully

The lies I began telling myself in those early years were powerful: *I'm too much and not enough at the same time. If people really knew me, they wouldn't accept me.* These lies were a way of shielding myself from the pain of rejection, but they didn't protect me. They kept me trapped in a cycle of shame, and as Proverbs 13:12 says, *"Hope deferred makes the heart sick."* It's no wonder I struggled with loving myself. How could I, when I believed the lies that I wasn't worthy?

I escaped into my own fantasy world, one where I could pretend the hurt wasn't there. But over time, I came to realize that those fantasies didn't heal me. They only kept me disconnected from my true self and from God's love.

## A Spiritual Transformation

At twenty-eight, I went through an emotional breakdown. Looking back, I can now see that what truly broke was not just my emotional stability, but my illusions. I had been trying to fix myself, to mask the hurt, to find healing on my own. But I couldn't. As Brené Brown (2013) wisely puts it, what I experienced wasn't just a breakdown, it was a spiritual transformation.

Spiritual transformation isn't about trying harder or doing more; it's about letting go of the illusions that we can fix ourselves and allowing God to do the healing. It requires vulnerability, courage to name the wounds, to confront the lies, and to invite God's love into the darkest places of our hearts.

Healing isn't quick or easy, but it is possible. And it starts with embracing God's love for us, love that is not based on our performance or worthiness but on His grace.

## Closing Thoughts

As I continue on this journey, I've learned that love is the key to transformation. It's not about trying harder; it's about surrendering more deeply. It's about accepting the love God has for us, even when we don't feel worthy, and letting that love change us from the inside out.

A threshold is crossed when we say yes to love, again and again. When we allow God's love to rewrite the story that we've been telling ourselves. And when we surrender our shame, the love of God rises and transforms us, making us whole again.

Love is the way home.

But love doesn't only touch the heart, the mind, or the soul, it reaches all the way into our bodies. For many of us, trauma has not only left emotional and spiritual scars but physical ones too. Our bodies remember what our minds try to forget. They hold pain, tension, and sometimes deep shame.

As we continue this journey of healing, we now turn to the wounds carried in our physical selves, the places where trauma, illness, or chronic stress have left their mark. What does it mean to care for a body that has been hurt or betrayed? How do we begin to listen to the wisdom of our bodies, rather than silencing them with busyness, fear, or disconnection?

In the next chapter, we'll explore how God meets us in our physical pain, how healing can be both spiritual and embodied, and how, through honouring our bodies, we learn to live more fully, more freely, in the grace we've been given.

---

## Declarations

I declare that God's love is greater than my wounds, and His grace is rewriting every story shaped by shame and fear.

I declare that I am being healed and transformed as I learn to love God with all my heart, soul, mind, and strength.

I declare that my past does not define me, God's love restores my identity and renews my capacity to give and receive love.

I declare that I am no longer bound by the lies of unworthiness; I am deeply known, fully accepted, and fiercely loved by God.

I declare that love is my calling, my healing, and my home, and I will walk in it, even when it costs me, because love never fails.

---

## Prayer

*Lord God,*
*You see every wound I carry; those hidden deep within and those that still ache with memory. You call me to love You with all my heart, soul, mind, and strength, yet so often, I feel too broken to respond. So I come to You, just as I am. Heal the places where love has been distorted by pain. Restore what has been stolen by shame. Teach me to trust again, to open my heart fully, and to live as one who is deeply loved.*

*I surrender the lies I've believed and the masks I've worn. Fill me with Your Spirit and transform me from the inside out. Let Your love be the foundation of my life and the overflow of my heart. Make me whole, O God, and help me to love as You love. In Jesus' name, Amen.*

---

## Reflection Questions

1. What has love looked like for me in seasons of pain or brokenness?
2. In what areas of my life do I find it hardest to receive God's love fully?
3. How have my wounds shaped the way I love others, or the way I protect myself from love?
4. What does it mean to me that love doesn't erase my history but rewrites my story?
5. Where might God be inviting me to show up with gentleness, for myself, for someone else, or for Him?
6. What does it look like, in this season, to say 'yes' to love, especially when it's hard?

---

## Journal Prompt

Write or draw a short prayer or reflection: Where is God inviting me to say yes to love today, even in the places that still feel wounded or hard to reach? Let your pen move without censoring. See what flows out.

# CHAPTER 4

## *My Body Remembers*

---

*"Stop treating your wound like it's something you imagined. If you see the wound is real, then you can heal it."*
*~ Bardugo, (2017), Crooked Kingdom*

*"Just as physical wounds heal at different rates in different people, so do emotional wounds. Everyone has different needs and speeds." ~ Karen Salmansohn*

*"Have mercy on me, Lord, for I am faint; heal me, Lord, for my bones are in agony. My soul is in deep anguish. How long, Lord, how long? Turn, Lord, and deliver me; save me because of your unfailing love." ~ Psalm 6:2-4*

---

### When The Body Carries What The Heart Can't Say

Pain doesn't just live in our thoughts or feelings; it settles into our bodies. Even when we think we've moved on, our bodies often carry the residue of what we've lived through. A tightness in the chest. A clenched jaw. A sudden fatigue we can't explain. Sometimes, without warning, a smell or a sound will send us spiralling, not because we're weak, but because our bodies remember what our minds have tried to forget.

I used to think healing was mostly about changing how I

thought or what I believed. But I've learned, sometimes the hard way, that our healing must also include our bodies. That the Spirit of God doesn't just want to renew our minds or lift our souls, but to dwell with us in the flesh-and-bone places where trauma has left its mark.

In this chapter, we'll explore how God meets us in the hidden pain our bodies carry, and how honouring that pain with compassion can become the beginning of deep, embodied healing.

## The Broken Strong

In 2003, I published a peer-reviewed article exploring the connection between body and mind (adapted from Davis, 2015). At the time, I suspected a link between my own experience of physical meningitis and what I later came to call *"meningitis of the soul."* The connection seemed almost too obvious to ignore. This chapter explores the intersection of physical pain and inner wounding, inviting us to consider how the body often speaks what the soul cannot yet say.

Helen Flanders Dunbar (1943, 1947), an American psychoanalyst, was pivotal in popularizing the term "psychosomatic" in the 1940s and 1950s. She proposed that the symptoms of any illness often reflect deeper, emotional wounds. I found myself thinking of this when I spoke with my adult son, who had recently dislocated his shoulder. At the time, he was going through an emotional upheaval, an inner dislocation that mirrored his physical injury. The connection between the two was striking and undeniably real.

I've long been drawn to body-oriented therapeutic approaches, which suggest that our bodies store the memories of pain (Ogden, Minton & Pain, 2006). During my doctoral research, I worked with war-traumatized populations, where many survivors of severe trauma reported bodily symptoms like stomach aches, symptoms that masked deeper emotional or psychological wounds. Rather than presenting with recognizable signs of depression or PTSD, they presented with pain that was far more tangible and physical.

Neurobiology supports this, confirming that the brain sometimes fails to process overwhelming traumatic events, causing the trauma's undischarged energy to be stored in the body as *"body memories"* (Fisher, 2009). When individuals encounter stimuli reminiscent of the original trauma, say, a smell, sound, or colour, they can be flooded with memories and emotions. It's as if the body is holding onto these memories for us, dragging us back to the place of pain, where the wound was first inflicted. The physiological roots of trauma are profound. A threshold is crossed when we meet our body's pain with compassion.

## Why Some Rise And Others Break

The year before I contracted meningitis, I went through a series of seismic disappointments, losses, disillusionments, and painful surprises that, when added together, brought me to a breaking point. Individually, each event might not have been overwhelming, but cumulatively, they created a profound emotional inflammation.

At the time, I wondered if I would ever feel normal again. It felt as though something inside me had irreparably broken. There was no quick fix, no comforting word, no medicine that could ease the throbbing in my mind, my soul, and my spirit. I had to ride it out. The swelling of grief and sorrow seemed relentless. Would body-oriented therapy have helped? Or soul work? Or spiritual intervention? How does one recover from *"meningitis of the soul,"* when the emotional inflammation lingers far longer than expected? And when the soul itself feels fractured, what can we do?

We often ask: What makes some people emerge from hardships stronger while others spiral into bitterness? Are challenges truly the work of the enemy, or could they be doorways that lead to greater resilience? Does wisdom grow from vulnerability? I've often wondered if it's true that struggle builds resilience, deepens our vision, and transforms the spirit. It's a question that can only be answered in the context of experience.

Pain has a strange way of unearthing what we value most, often in the most uncomfortable ways. When life crumbles, we're forced to confront our lack of control over what matters to us most. The illusion that life will be easy shatters, and we must face the reality of our vulnerability. The grieving process is one of relinquishing dreams and hopes. Sometimes we're called to let go of the life we thought we would have, the dreams that gave us comfort.

It's interesting that the first step in the Twelve Step Recovery Program (Alcoholics Anonymous World Services, Inc., 2002) is admitting our powerlessness. For me, this resonates with the experience of trauma, where we are forced to face that we are powerless over events outside our control. How does one emerge from overwhelming loss and find strength?

## Who Becomes Resilient?

The question of resilience often points back to emotional muscle. Like a physical muscle, our emotional resilience grows with use. I've noticed that those who face the deepest crises, like those in the aftermath of September 11 in America, seem better equipped to handle trauma. They appear more flexible, able to adjust to life's unpredictability. In contrast, those who have lived with fewer trials tend to struggle more when the rug is pulled out from under them. Resilience isn't simply about surviving; it's about growing stronger in the face of adversity.

This concept of resilience was constantly at play in my work as a trauma counsellor. As a wounded healer (Nouwen, 1979), I spent years working with survivors of war in northern Uganda and northern Sri Lanka. I began to see how profound trauma shatters not just the body, but a person's sense of self, their safety, and their ability to control their world. It's a humbling thing to witness how the brokenness becomes a source of new strength for some, while others are trapped in the chaos of their unresolved pain.

Trauma, especially when inflicted on a collective level, is a hard teacher. It strips a person down to their rawest vulnerability. And yet, what I have learned through years of working with survivors is that strength is often birthed in brokenness. Many survivors share that the key to recovery is opening up, to let others into their pain and give voice to their wounds. This is one of the most difficult, and often the most healing, steps in the journey.

For many of us, we are taught to hide our wounds. I was raised in a culture that valued strength as emotional control, especially in times of grief or hardship. It's a paradox: we are told that we are weak if we show emotion, and yet, it is in our most broken moments that we discover strength we never knew we had.

In my case, my meningitis healed physically long before my soul found peace. It was an extraordinary process, one of surrender, of allowing the pain to teach me something deeper. I'm still learning how to handle life's crises with less drama, but in this journey of brokenness, I continue to find my strength, piece by piece.

## The God Who Heals

Jesus played a central role in healing physical wounds during His ministry. The name Jehovah-Rapha, meaning *"the God who heals,"* speaks to God's deep desire to restore wholeness to His people. But as we see throughout the Gospels, Jesus' healing wasn't just about restoring the physical body; it was about holistic restoration, body, soul, and spirit.

In the New Testament, the Greek words for healing give us further insight into the breadth of God's desire to heal:

1. **Sozo**: This word speaks to complete salvation and restoration. While it includes physical healing, its primary focus is on spiritual restoration and deliverance. Jesus' healing ministry encompasses the total well-being of the person (Isaiah 53:5) (Strong, 1995).
2. **Therapeuo**: From which we derive the word *"therapy,"* this term refers to treating and serving the sick. Jesus demonstrated His compassion by healing physical ailments (Thayer, 1989).
3. **Iaomai**: A more immediate, miraculous form of healing, this word often refers to divine intervention and freedom from oppression, as seen in the many instances where Jesus casts out demons and heals the body (Thayer, 1989).

Jesus' healing ministry wasn't just about fixing bodies; it was about making people whole, emotionally, spiritually, and physically. One of the most striking examples of this is the healing of the woman bent over for eighteen years in Luke 13:10-17. Jesus recognized that her physical ailment was connected to spiritual oppression. He healed both the body and the spirit, freeing her from bondage and restoring her to health.

This story is a powerful reminder that the mind, body, and spirit are interconnected. Jesus came to heal the whole person, offering not only physical restoration but also freedom from spiritual and emotional bondage.

## Closing Thoughts

Jesus offers us the fullness of healing, not just in our bodies, but in our souls and spirits as well. His love and grace call us to embrace a holistic restoration, one that invites us to become whole again, so that His life can be lived fully in and through us.

But healing doesn't stop at the surface. If our bodies carry the impact of trauma, our minds often carry the weight of it, the distorted beliefs, the anxious thoughts, the mental scripts formed in pain and self-protection. These wounds of the mind can be just as limiting, just as exhausting, and just as in need of grace.

In the next chapter, we turn toward the tender and sometimes tangled space of the mind, where toxic thoughts take root, where lies can masquerade as truth, and where the battle for peace is often fought. Healing our minds means learning to recognize the patterns that keep us bound and opening ourselves to God's renewing truth. Because when the mind begins to heal, clarity returns. Hope rises. And we begin to see ourselves, and God, with fresh eyes.

---

## Declarations

I declare that You, Heavenly Father, are Jehovah Rapha, my Healer and I thank You. I stand on the truth of Your Word in Jeremiah 30:17: *"For I will restore health to you, and your wounds I will heal, declares the Lord."* I declare that this promise is alive and active in my life and the lives of my family.

I declare in the name of Jesus Christ, that every stronghold that seeks to affect my physical health and well-being is broken. I declare complete healing and restoration in every area of my body. Your Word says that Jesus Himself took our infirmities and bore our sicknesses (Matthew 8:17). Therefore, I boldly proclaim that by His wounds, I am healed (1 Peter 2:24).

I declare that I reject any curse of physical injury, sickness, or disease, and I claim the redemptive power of Jesus' sacrifice over my life and my family. Thank You, Lord, for Your faithfulness, for Your healing touch, and for the authority of Your Word.

I declare wholeness, health, and divine protection over myself and my family in the beautiful and mighty name of Jesus. All glory and honour belong to You, Lord. Amen.

---

## Prayer

*Blessed Jesus,*
*In the comfort of your love, I lay before you the memories that haunt me, the anxieties that perplex me, the despair that frightens me, and my frustration at my inability to think clearly. Help me to discover your forgiveness in my memories and know your peace in my distress. Touch my physical body where trauma is stored, O Lord, and fill me with your light and your hope. Amen.*
(Adapted from *Healing from the Past*, Church Publishing, 2000).

---

## Reflection Questions

1. As you reflect on your own life, where do you feel the pain of unhealed wounds, whether physical, emotional, or spiritual?
2. In what ways do you feel God inviting you into a deeper healing?
3. Write down a prayer acknowledging the areas of your life that need His touch of restoration.

---

## Journal Prompt

Write or draw a short prayer or reflection: Where in my life, body, mind, or spirit, is God inviting me to receive His healing and become whole? Let your pen move without censoring. See what flows out.

# CHAPTER 5

## *When My Thoughts Become Wounds*

---

*"You cannot have a positive life and a negative mind." ~ Joyce Meyer*

*"The mind is not a vessel to be filled but a fire to be kindled." ~ Plutarch*

*"Do not conform to the pattern of this world but be transformed by the renewing of your mind." ~ Romans 12:2*

---

### The Mind's Hidden Wounds

While my body carries the imprints of past wounds, it is often my thoughts that keep those wounds alive. Long after the event has passed, a word, a memory, or an internal accusation can open a fresh tear in my soul. I've come to see that trauma doesn't only settle in the muscles or nervous system, it weaves its way into the mind, distorting truth, shaping belief, and fuelling shame. As I began to listen more closely to the stories my thoughts were telling me, I realized they, too, needed healing. And so, we turn toward the landscape of our minds, where pain often disguises itself as reason, and begin the slow work of renewal.

So much of my spiritual life was shaped by what I thought I

was supposed to believe. I had been a Christian for decades, read Scripture faithfully, taught others, counselled those in deep distress, and witnessed God's grace redeem horrific suffering. Yet somehow, I had learned to carry my own mental anguish alone, as if it were mine to manage in private. The unspoken assumption: *I'm too damaged to heal.*

But pain has a way of forcing us to pay attention. When the mind is fractured by lies, old agreements, or the unresolved wounds of trauma, the soul knows something is off. We may not know how to name it yet, but God does. And He is not put off by our confusion. He is already drawing near. For years, my mind kept rehearsing pain. I didn't know it could be a sanctuary of peace, a place where God would meet me, not to shame me, but to heal me.

## Loving God With A Wounded Mind

*"Love the Lord your God with all your heart, with all your soul, with all your mind, and with all your strength."* This command from Jesus has always intrigued me. How do we love God with our mind, especially when our mind has been wounded? When our thoughts betray us, or when our internal world is filled with confusion, condemnation, or fear? For many, the mind becomes a battlefield. But for those who carry unhealed wounds from the past, it can feel like the mind has become enemy territory.

The wounds we carry in our minds often run deeper than we realise. They are not always visible like scars on the body, yet they shape how we think, how we interpret the world, and how we relate to others and to God. These mind wounds are formed when we are overwhelmed by life's painful experiences, especially when those experiences leave us feeling powerless, confused, or abandoned. For me, the journey of healing these inner wounds has been both deeply personal and profoundly spiritual.

## Awakening To The Inner Landscape

I still remember the night I sat in my room, trembling with emotion. I'd just returned from Sri Lanka, where I'd been working with war-affected communities, students, nurses, teachers, and church leaders still aching from decades of ethnic war. Their suffering had touched me deeply. I had absorbed more than I realised. The sights, the stories, the silent grief etched into faces, I carried it all home with me.

Re-entry into my 'normal' life felt disorienting. I was jet-lagged, vulnerable, and still carrying the ache of the people I had left behind. Then, just days later, a painful confrontation with a loved one caught me off guard. Their words pierced deeper than they intended, hitting raw, unguarded places in me. It wasn't just about what was said, it was the feeling of being unseen, misjudged, and emotionally ambushed at a time when I was least able to defend myself. I froze. My body went cold, my mind fogged over, and I couldn't speak. I was engulfed in sorrow, confused and distant, as if part of me had gone numb to survive.

It was only later that I realised what had happened: I had been triggered. The emotional weight I had carried from the field, combined with a moment of relational rupture, had reactivated older wounds, wounds of not feeling safe, of being misunderstood, of longing for connection but fearing rejection. It awakened something deeper in me, something that had been quietly simmering in the background for years.

## Recognizing The Voice Of The Enemy

As I sat with the pain, I began to notice the script playing in my head. Words like: *You're too much. You're not enough. You're difficult to love.* The harshness of those words stunned me. They weren't new. They were old echoes, embedded in the neural pathways of my brain, beliefs formed in childhood, reinforced over time, and now awakened in the midst of present-day sorrow.

The voice in my mind mimicked truth. It used my own voice. But it was laced with shame and accusation. It pointed to evidence from my past and whispered that nothing would ever change. It was so familiar I hadn't questioned it.

But as I leaned into prayer, I sensed something else: a gentle nudge from the Holy Spirit revealing that this voice was not neutral. It was a strategic assault, an internalised lie, a mind wound that had become a stronghold.

## Mind Wounds And The Way Of Trauma

Trauma lives in the body and speaks through the mind. As Bessel van der Kolk (1994) describes, *"The body keeps the score."* But our thoughts, how we make sense of what's happened, often keep the story going. They become internal narratives that drive fear, shame, self-blame, or hopelessness. They distort reality, trap us in cycles of defensiveness or despair, and can even shape how we see God.

Trauma disrupts the integration of our experiences. What was once a safe space may suddenly feel threatening. We might react to current situations as if the past were happening all over again, especially when the original pain happened in relationships. And that's the cruel irony: the places we most long for love and connection are often the places where pain has written its deepest script.

## The Need For Secure Attachment

Every child is wired for connection. We long to be seen, soothed, safe, and secure. But when caregivers are emotionally unavailable, dismissive, or unpredictable, we adapt. We may become hyper-vigilant, compliant, or shut down. We internalize the pain and make it about ourselves. The resulting beliefs: *I'm not lovable, I must perform to be accepted, and My needs don't matter,* don't stay in childhood. They follow us into adulthood, into our relationships, and into our relationship with God.

Loving God with all our mind requires that we allow the Spirit to transform these internalized lies. It's not enough to cognitively affirm that God loves us. Our wounded parts must experience that love in ways that feel safe, true, and healing.

## Attachment Trauma And Relationships

Understanding intergenerational trauma through an attachment lens has helped me recognise how it shaped not only my own struggles but also those of my children. The ability to attune to others is foundational for feeling safe and connected. I still remember the deep helplessness I felt when I couldn't soothe my infant daughter. She cried endlessly, and I had no idea how to respond.

Years later, I learned about research showing that mothers with unresolved trauma often show atypical brain responses to their infant's distress, resulting in misattunement (Iyengar et al., 2014). In hindsight, my inability to respond to my children's emotional needs reflected my own inner child, still crying out in vain.

Trauma's legacy ripples through generations. Even into their thirties, my children wrestled with insecure attachment styles shaped by my unresolved pain. Their struggles with emotional regulation, intimacy, and identity were devastating to witness. And as a mother, I bore the sting of rejection and blame. Their pain eclipsed my own. My nervous system lived in hypervigilance. I retreated, disconnected, just as I had in childhood, and in doing so, I deepened their pain.

I grieved. I condemned myself. I felt crushed by the weight of my perceived failure. What parent can prepare for the grief of watching their children flail through the consequences of inherited wounds?

## Making Sense Of Suffering

Ironically, my work as a trauma counsellor felt like a divine fit. Bearing witness to unspeakable suffering in war zones, I often found myself in parallel anguish, grappling with both global pain and personal heartache. I gave voice to the silenced, and they somehow recognised that I carried their pain too.

Still, I wrestled with the tension between God's promises and the reality of suffering. Why would God allow this? And how could pain possibly be part of His plan?

C.S. Lewis famously wrote that *"pain is God's megaphone."* But what we hear depends on how we relate to the One who speaks. Again and again, God asked me to trust Him. But trust was hard. My life-long trauma responses, hypervigilance, self-protection, control, revealed just how difficult trust had become.

## Coping As Control

One day, it hit me: my coping was actually control. And control was killing me. I wasn't just reacting; I was resisting surrender. And the cost was written in my body: inflammation, exhaustion, disconnection. I had buried my pain alive, hoping it would stay quiet. But it never does.

So, I repented. I grieved. Not just what happened to me, but the way I had responded, with self-protection instead of surrender. And then, I sought therapy. I found a body-oriented therapist specialising in EMDR (Eye Movement Desensitization and Reprocessing). After the first session, I came home and slept for an hour in the middle of the day. It was like my body finally exhaled. I booked another session. And another. And something beautiful happened.

As I gained my emotional footing, I began creating spaces for others to heal. I started hosting small groups with friends, where we could speak truth, sit in silence, and listen deeply. We became more attuned, more compassionate, toward others and ourselves.

Healing the mind takes time. But it's possible. And it always leads back to connection: with God, with others, and with the self we've been hiding for so long.

## Healing Through Encounter

God does not shame us for our brokenness. He meets us in it. Often gently. One night, in the thick of emotional pain, I cried out to God: *"Why do I shut down like this? Why can't I speak?"* I expected silence. Maybe rebuke. Instead, I sensed the whisper: " *Because you weren't heard when you were little."*

That truth pierced me, not in judgment, but in love. I saw the little girl in me, frightened, unheard, hiding. And I saw Jesus beside her, not demanding change, but offering presence.
This is how a fragile hope awakened: not with striving, but with encounter.

## Renewing The Mind With Truth

Paul wrote, *"Do not be conformed to the pattern of this world but be transformed by the renewing of your mind"* (Romans 12:2). That kind of transformation doesn't happen overnight. It's a process. A partnership with the Spirit.

Truth doesn't always shout. Sometimes it's a whisper. A friend's kindness. A moment of rest. A verse that lands differently. It anchors us to the character of God: that He is for us. That we are His. That nothing, no pain, no wound, is beyond redemption.

## Moving Forward: An Invitation To Awareness

If the mind is a battlefield, awareness is our first defence. Begin noticing the voices in your head. Are they kind or condemning? Do they sound like Jesus, or do they echo shame? Ask yourself: Whose voice is this?

You do not have to be held hostage by old thought patterns. Neural pathways can be rewired. Strongholds can be torn down. The dark can start to loosen its hold. And truth begins with noticing.

## You Are Not Alone

Your mind is a precious part of how you love God. He does not despise your struggle. He longs to restore every wounded place. So, ask Him: Where have I believed lies? Where do I need to grieve? Where do I need to surrender?

He will meet you there. He always does. *"I sought the Lord, and he answered me; he delivered me from all my fears"* (Psalm 34:4).

## Reflection Practices

To help you deepen this journey, here are some practices to try:

- **Daily Mind Check-In**: Take five minutes each day to notice your inner dialogue. Jot down any recurring thoughts. Are they rooted in truth or fear?
- **Compassionate Self-Talk**: Practice speaking to yourself as you would to a beloved child. What does that voice sound like?
- **Scripture Meditation**: Choose one verse that reminds you of God's truth about you (for example, Romans 8:1, Psalm 139:14). Let it sink into your heart and mind.
- **Dialogue with God**: Write a letter to God about your mind wounds. Then, listen in prayer for what He might want to say in return.

## Closing Thoughts

Let this be the invitation at the close of this chapter, not just to know more about healing, but to experience it. Not just to read about mind renewal, but to taste it, even now.

But healing, especially in the realm of the mind, also invites us into complexity. Into the layered, intricate workings of thought, emotion, memory, and meaning making. As we continue this journey, it becomes important to pause, not to fix or simplify, but to understand. To hold the complexity of the mind with reverence, rather than fear. To explore the theories and frameworks that help us make sense of how our minds have been shaped by trauma, attachment, culture, and neurobiology.

This next chapter invites us into that sacred space, where spiritual insight and psychological understanding meet. Where we honour both the mystery and the mechanics of the mind, trusting that God is present in both. Because to heal deeply, we must not only feel, we must also understand. And in that understanding, we begin to partner with God in the renewing of our minds.

---

## Declarations

I declare that I am being *"...renewed in the spirit of [my] mind"* (Ephesians 4:23).

I declare that I am full of the mercy of God and not trapped by my thoughts. The truth is what God says.

I declare that at this very moment I am seated with Him in heavenly places. I declare that I will trust my future to Jesus and continually remind myself of His loving-kindness toward me.

---

## Prayer

Take a few moments in stillness. You might want to place a hand over your heart. Let your body settle. Then read and pray slowly:

*Jesus, I invite You into the hidden places of my mind, the places where I still believe lies, where shame has built strongholds, where old pain echoes louder than Your truth.*
*I want to love You with all my mind. I want my thoughts to reflect Your goodness, Your kindness, Your hope.*
*Where I've rehearsed fear, teach me to practice trust.*
*Where I've absorbed shame, speak Your delight over me.*
*Where I've tried to control, help me to surrender.*
*Show me what is true.*
*I am Yours.*
*Renew my mind, Lord, and anchor it in Your love.*
*Amen.*

---

## Reflection Questions

### Listening for the Lie, Inviting the Truth

1. *Name the Lie*
   Ask the Spirit to gently reveal one untrue belief you've been holding.

*"What have I been believing about myself that isn't true?"*
Write it down.

2. *Notice the Origin*
   Ask,

*"When did I first begin to believe this?"*
*"What was happening in my life?"*
Be kind to yourself as memories or emotions surface.

3. *Invite Jesus into That Place*

Picture Him there with you, in the memory, in the pain.
What is His posture toward you?
What is He saying?

4. *Replace the Lie with His Truth*
   Ask,

*"Jesus, what do You want me to know instead?"*
Let His truth settle deep in you. Write it somewhere visible.

---

## Journal Prompt

Write or draw a short prayer or reflection: "Loving God with my mind looks like..." Let your pen move without censoring. See what flows out.

# CHAPTER 6

## *Holding Complexity in My Story*

---

*"The mind is like the stomach. It is not how much you put into it that counts, but how much it digests." ~ Albert J. Nock*

*"For as he thinks within himself, so he is." ~ Proverbs 23:7*

---

### The Mind: Battlefield, Belief, And Becoming

The mind is not just a thinking machine. It is a field of battle, a place of belief, a vault of memories, a theatre of imagination, and often, a sanctuary or a prison, depending on who has access to it.

In this chapter, I want to hold space for the many ways we've come to understand the mind, scientifically, psychologically, biblically, and reflect on how trauma, healing, and spiritual transformation are not merely processes of the soul or body but deeply rooted in the mind's terrain.

### Theories Of The Mind: A Biblical Perspective

In the journey of trauma recovery, one of the most crucial aspects of healing is understanding how the mind works, how it is shaped by past experiences, how it reacts in the present, and how it can be transformed through the work of the Holy Spirit.

As someone who has spent years in the field of trauma counselling, I've seen firsthand how the mind can become a battleground. And, in my own life, I've experienced the deep struggle between the thoughts and emotions that arise from trauma and the truth that God desires to renew and restore my mind.

Secular theories of the mind, often focusing on cognitive processes, emotional regulation, and behaviour, offer valuable insights into the way we think and act. Yet, as a Christian, I've come to believe that these theories, though helpful, are incomplete without the larger framework of God's Word. The secular understanding of the mind can describe what happens in the brain and the nervous system, but it falls short of addressing the deeper, spiritual dimension of the human experience. Trauma touches not just the brain and body but also the soul, and it's only through a biblical understanding of the mind that we can hope to experience true healing.

## 1. A Spiritual Lens For Understanding Trauma

To understand the mind from a biblical perspective, we must begin by recognizing that the mind is not just a cognitive mechanism but is deeply intertwined with our identity and relationship with God. In Scripture, the mind is often described as the seat of understanding, wisdom, and discernment (Proverbs 2:6, Romans 12:2). It's where our thoughts, beliefs, and desires are formed, and it's also where our struggle with sin and brokenness takes place. In the context of trauma, the mind is not just affected by the event itself but by the way we process, internalize, and interpret those events.

As I've worked with trauma survivors, I've seen how deeply traumatic experiences can distort the way a person perceives themselves, others, and the world around them. A person who has been abused, for example, may carry with them a belief that they are unworthy of love or that the world is an unsafe place. These beliefs, formed in the mind, shape how they interact with others and how they see God. In this way, trauma doesn't just wound the body, it wounds the mind, leading to distorted thinking and emotional turmoil.

However, the Bible offers hope. Through Christ, we are offered the possibility of a new mind, one that is transformed by the renewing power of the Holy Spirit (Romans 12:2). This renewal doesn't just happen through behaviour modification or cognitive therapy. It happens as we bring our wounded minds before God, allowing Him to speak truth into the lies that have shaped our perception. As Isaiah 26:3 says, *"You keep him in perfect peace whose mind is stayed on you, because he trusts in you."* (Psalm 51:10).

## 2. Theories Of The Mind In Secular Psychology

Secular psychology offers valuable tools for understanding the cognitive and emotional effects of trauma. One of the most well-known models in trauma therapy is the cognitive-behavioural approach, which focuses on identifying and changing distorted thought patterns that contribute to emotional distress and maladaptive behaviours. In this model, trauma survivors are encouraged to challenge their negative beliefs and replace them with more rational, balanced thoughts. For example, a person who believes *"I am worthless"* might be encouraged to reframe that thought to *"I am valuable, and my worth is not based on my experiences."*

While this approach can be helpful, especially for individuals seeking relief from anxiety, depression, and post-traumatic stress, it is limited in that it does not address the deeper spiritual wounds that often accompany trauma. For many trauma survivors, cognitive changes alone are insufficient. Healing requires more than just a change in thought patterns, it requires a transformation of the heart, which, in the Christian faith, is deeply tied to our relationship with God.

Another widely recognized theory of the mind in trauma recovery is the emotional regulation model, which focuses on how individuals manage their emotions in response to distressing events. This model highlights the importance of emotional awareness and the ability to self-soothe in times of crisis. The idea is that trauma survivors often experience heightened emotional reactivity, and learning to regulate these emotions is key to healing. Techniques such as mindfulness, grounding exercises, and breathing techniques are used to help individuals regain a sense of control over their emotional responses.

While these tools can be beneficial, they again fall short of addressing the spiritual dimension of emotional healing. Emotional regulation can certainly help an individual manage overwhelming feelings, but it does not necessarily bring lasting peace or restoration. This is where the role of faith becomes crucial. When we are able to surrender our emotional pain to God and invite His peace into our hearts, emotional healing can move beyond mere self-regulation to true spiritual transformation.

## 3. The Role Of The Brain And Nervous System In Trauma

The field of neuroscience has given us a deeper understanding of how trauma impacts the brain and nervous system. Trauma survivors often experience a dysregulation of the autonomic nervous system, leading to symptoms such as hypervigilance, heightened stress response, and difficulty calming down after being triggered. Brain imaging studies have shown that traumatic experiences can alter the structure and function of the brain, particularly in areas related to memory, fear, and emotional processing (Henigsberg et al., 2019; Neria et al., 2024).

In my work with survivors, I've witnessed how these changes in the brain manifest in everyday life. A person who has experienced trauma may feel constantly on edge, even in situations where there is no immediate threat. Their nervous system is in a state of "fight or flight," making it difficult for them to relax or feel safe. This constant state of stress can lead to a host of physical and psychological symptoms, including chronic pain, insomnia, anxiety, and depression.

The good news, however, is that the brain is also capable of healing. Neuroplasticity, the brain's ability to reorganize itself and form new neural connections, offers hope for trauma recovery. Through practices such as mindfulness, EMDR, and trauma-informed therapies, the brain can begin to heal and rewire itself, creating new pathways for healthy emotional regulation and stress management.

But again, this healing is not purely a biological process. The biblical understanding of healing recognizes that the mind and body are deeply intertwined, and true healing comes when we bring both our physical and emotional wounds before God, allowing His healing touch to restore us in every aspect of our being.

## 4. Integrating Secular And Biblical Perspectives

In my own journey, I've found that integrating secular theories of the mind with biblical truth has been the most effective way to heal from trauma. The wisdom of secular psychology and neuroscience provides helpful tools for understanding the mechanisms of trauma, but it is the transformative power of God's Word and His Spirit that brings lasting healing.

As I continue to work with trauma survivors and reflect on my own healing process, I've come to believe that the true path to recovery lies in allowing God's Word to shape our understanding of ourselves and our circumstances. The theories of the mind, while useful, are incomplete without the profound truth that we are created in the image of God, that we are deeply loved by Him, and that our healing is ultimately a work of divine restoration.

This chapter is not just an exploration of theory; it is a call to action. It invites us to engage with both the wisdom of modern psychology and the timeless truths of Scripture as we seek to heal from trauma. Our minds may be wounded, but through the power of Christ, we can be transformed. And it is in this transformation that we find true healing, mind, body, and soul.

## Beck's Cognitive Triad: A Window Into The Wounded Mind

I still remember the weight of those dark days, the heaviness in my chest, the fog in my thinking, the persistent ache of believing something was fundamentally wrong with me. Depression was not just a passing cloud; it settled in like an unwelcome guest, distorting the way I saw myself, the world around me, and any possibility of a hopeful future.

Looking back, I see now how clearly my experience reflected Aaron Beck's Cognitive Triad, a model he proposed in 1967. Beck observed that those suffering from depression tend to hold a trio of distorted beliefs: a negative view of the self, the world, and the future. These aren't just passing thoughts; they stem from deep mental structures, schemas, formed by our earliest experiences and reinforced over time, especially during stress.

Beck's theory resonated with me not just intellectually but personally. I lived it. (See Figure 1. *Beck's Cognitive Triad*).

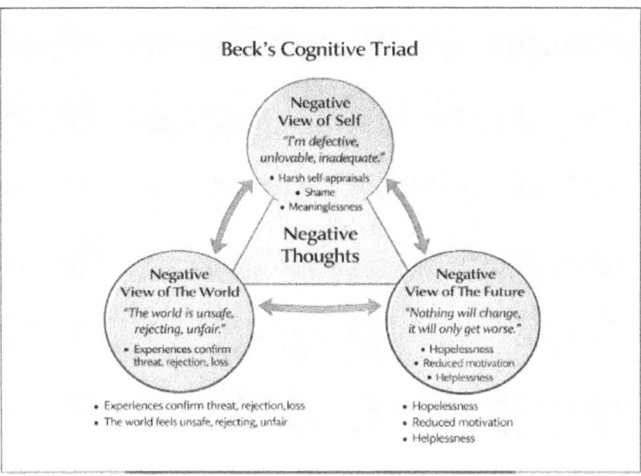


Figure 1. *Beck's Cognitive Triad*

## How Trauma Activates Deep Schemas

During my struggle with postnatal depression, I found myself tormented by a terrifying belief: my daughter didn't want me as her mother. At the time, her constant crying felt like rejection, confirming what my mind, already worn thin, was whispering in the shadows: *You're not enough... You're a failure.*

It sounds irrational now, but that's the deceptive power of trauma-triggered schemas. They lie in wait, often invisible until something painful awakens them. For me, that critical moment of becoming a mother activated long-buried assumptions I'd carried from childhood, messages shaped by rejection and criticism. One in particular stood out: *"Unless I am loved, I am worthless."*

This was the lens through which I viewed myself and my relationship with my newborn daughter. Beck's model helped me understand what was happening, that these automatic thoughts weren't coming from nowhere. They were erupting from deep wells of unresolved pain.

## Schemas In Everyday Life

These deep-rooted patterns stick with us into adulthood, subtly influencing how we understand others' actions and how we react in relationships. They especially come to the surface during times of stress and crisis.

Years later, I noticed this same schema re-emerge in my marriage. When my husband was deeply engaged in his work, I began to feel invisible, less important than the things that absorbed his attention. That old inner narrative, the one rooted in shame, began to replay: *"I'm not worth his time... I'm deeply flawed... if he really knew me, he'd withdraw."*

And so, rather than voicing my needs, I withdrew emotionally, reinforcing the very isolation I feared. These negative assumptions became a self-fulfilling prophecy. I wasn't responding to reality, but to the echo of old wounds.

Recognising these patterns was a breakthrough. It allowed me to begin challenging the cognitive distortions and identifying their origins. But more than that, it invited me into a deeper spiritual journey, one of healing, repentance, and renewal in the presence of God.

## From Cognitive Distortions To Truth

Below is a table of common negative messages and the emotional responses they generate. I invite you to reflect honestly as you read through them. Which messages have followed you into adulthood? Which ones feel uncomfortably familiar?

For me, message #6, *"You are flawed and inadequate"* was my shadow for many years. It shaped how I viewed conflict, how I handled disappointment, and how I interpreted love. These messages are powerful, not only because they feel true, but because they're often attached to formative relationships and experiences. By bringing these distortions into the light, we begin to loosen their grip. We create space for God's truth to take root.

| | MESSAGE | WHAT I TELL MYSELF NOW | RESPONSE |
|---|---|---|---|
| 1. | You are loved, wanted, and delighted in. | *"I am resilient and competent of giving and receiving love and connection. I can ask for help when needed. I trust those I love and am kind. I am hopeful that good things will come my way."* | Connection, affection, tenderness, compassion, warmth, joy, hopeful, elated, excited, happy |
| 2. | You don't matter. You are not important. | *"There is nobody there for me. I am on my own…"* | Hopelessness, empty, abandoned, rejected |
| 3. | You are insignificant and unworthy of connection. | *"I expect that I will lose anyone with whom I form an emotional attachment…"* | Intense fear, abandoned, rejected |
| 4. | You are disgusting and worthy of abuse. | *"People are out to get me… I expect that others will intentionally take advantage of me in some way… only I can look after me…"* | Separate, on-guard, strongly isolated, violated, against |
| 5. | You don't belong. Be invisible. | *"I am isolated from the world, different from other people, and not part of the community… I feel like an outsider… I will never fit in."* | Separate, disconnected, estranged, rejected, empty |
| 6. | You are flawed | *"I am internally* | Strong sense |

| | | | |
|---|---|---|---|
| | and inadequate. | *flawed and if others get close, they will realise this and withdraw from the relationship… I'll never be good enough…"* | of shame, core negativity |
| 7. | You are undesirable. | *"I am physically unattractive to others, socially inept and lack any status… I can see by the way they look at me."* | Core negativity, self-image of useless, wrong, stupid, undesirable, rejected |
| 8. | You are a failure. You will never achieve anything. | *"I am incapable of performing as well as my peers… I can't get it right… I am a failure…"* | stupid, inept, untalented, ignorant |
| 9. | You can't function independently from me. You are incompetent. | *"I am not capable of handling day-to-day responsibilities competently and independently. I must constantly rely on others for help."* | Intense insecurity, hesitancy to act without checking whether action is OK (parent figure often intrusive), enmeshed, disapproving, rejecting |
| 10. | Don't be a child. Be responsible. | *"I must take care of others. My needs don't count. Fun and play are frivolous."* | Frustration, anger, resentment |
| 11. | You are weak and inadequate. | *"I can't decide for myself because I'm* | Apprehension, fear, over- |

| | | | |
|---|---|---|---|
| | | *scared of making a mistake. I won't make any decisions; I will let others tell me what to do."* | whelmed, threatened |
| 12. | Don't be seen unless you are sick or naughty. | *"If I am constantly sick or display attention-seeking behaviour, I will get noticed."* | Sad, lonely, hurt, pity |
| 13. | Don't feel. You will get punished if you display feelings. | *"If I display any feelings the real me might come out and I am unacceptable."* | Despair, isolated, forlorn, detached, desolate |
| 14. | Don't be close. Keep distance between us and them. Don't talk to the neighbours. Don't trust anyone. | *"If I get too close to someone, or trust anyone because I will get hurt."* | Immobility, guilt, regretful, contrite |
| 15. | You are not worthy. | *"Something about me is lacking. I don't have what it takes, and my achievements don't count."* | Pain, depression, sad, lonely, hurt, pity, rage |
| 16. | Don't be you. I really wanted a boy/girl but got you instead. | *"No matter what I do, I will never be accepted. Something about me is unacceptable."* | Abandoned, unworthy, despair, desolate |
| 17. | I wish you had never been born. You are | *"I have no right to exist. I cause hurt and trouble wher-* | Depression, hopeless, powerless, sui- |

| | | | |
|---|---|---|---|
| | the cause of all the problems around here. | *ever I go. If things get too much for me, I will kill myself and cease to exist."* | cidal, shameful, rejected |
| 18. | Never grow up because I couldn't handle it. You will always be my little boy/girl. | *"I will remain a good, helpless, little boy or girl, that way nothing will be required of me, and I won't be rejected."* | Helpless, hopeless, powerless, angry |

*Table 1*. Messages & Responses

## Why CBT Isn't Always Enough

Beck's work laid the foundation for Cognitive Behavioral Therapy (CBT), a widely respected, evidence-based approach for treating depression. And it *is* effective, especially when paired with medication. But despite its strengths, research shows that two out of three people relapse into depression within two years of completing CBT. That statistic has always caught my attention.

CBT helped me recognise and reframe my negative cognitions. It offered tools for identifying unhelpful thought patterns and practicing more adaptive responses. But in the end, dismantling deeply entrenched thought strongholds felt like something more than a psychological task. It felt like a spiritual battle.

For me, true transformation required something CBT couldn't fully offer: the power of the Holy Spirit. I needed more than new thoughts; I needed a renewed mind. A mind no longer ruled by shame or fear, but anchored in the truth of who God says I am. And that kind of healing doesn't come from insight alone. It comes through repentance, surrender, and the Spirit's gentle work of restoration. It's not just about reprogramming the mind; it's about inviting God to inhabit it.

## Rational Emotive Behavioral Therapy (REBT)

Albert Ellis introduced Rational Emotive Behavior Therapy (REBT) in 1955, offering a revolutionary way to understand emotional responses. At its core, REBT proposes that it's not the events in our lives that disturb us, but how we interpret them. Ellis structured this insight into a simple, powerful model:

1. **Activating Event** - the situation, thought, or image that sparks a reaction
2. **Belief About the Event** - the meaning or interpretation we assign
3. **Emotional or Behavioural Consequence** - the resulting feeling or action

In other words, the problem is not the event itself, but the belief we attach to it (see Figure 2: *ABCs of Events*). What often goes unnoticed is how deeply embedded these beliefs are. They operate beneath our awareness, shaping our emotional lives and behaviour as if they were absolute truth. And unless we pause and challenge them, we'll keep rehearsing them, over and over, for the rest of our lives.

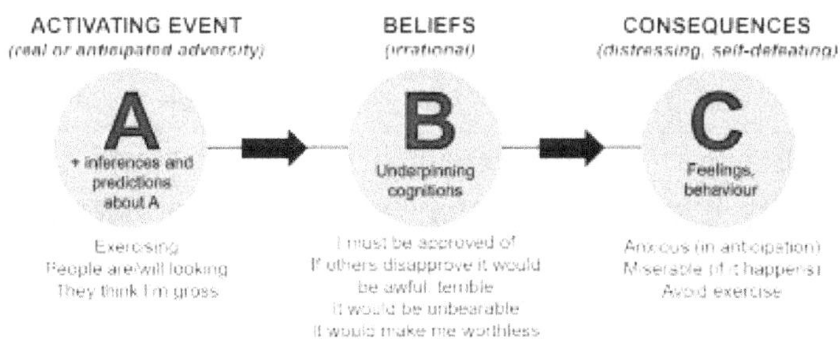


Figure 2. *ABC's of Events*

## When Beliefs Dictate The Story: Elliott's Reaction

To illustrate this, let me introduce you to my friend Elliott. One afternoon, Elliott came home from work and was blindsided by his wife's announcement: she was leaving him for someone else. Now, how might someone respond to such devastating news?

1. **Depression:** *"I'll never find someone as wonderful as her. I'm a loser."*
2. **Anger:** *"That #!@&% has no right to leave. I've given her everything."*
3. ***Relief or Happiness:*** *"Thank God she's leaving. I'll be rid of a big problem. Now I can get on with my life."*

Each of these emotional responses stems from a different belief system. For example:

- Depression might be driven by the belief: *"I'm unlovable, and my worth depends on being loved by others."*
- Anger might come from: *"People must treat me fairly, and if they don't, they deserve to be punished."*
- Happiness might be based on: *"Challenges bring new opportunities. I'll be okay."*

The same event. Three vastly different outcomes. The key difference? The beliefs behind them.

## Recognizing The Lies We Tell Ourselves

Ellis emphasized the importance of identifying and challenging these deeply ingrained beliefs. He developed a list of common cognitive distortions that shape our emotional responses (see *Table 2: REBT Beliefs*). As you read through them, you might recognize some of your own.

For instance, I resonate deeply with *catastrophising*. I've often caught myself exaggerating the weight of a single conversation or disagreement, especially with my teenage daughter. One small moment would snowball into a narrative of worst-case scenarios, flooding me with emotion. In those moments, my thinking brain would shut down. I couldn't be present. I wasn't solving problems; I was collapsing under the emotional weight of my beliefs. It was deeply disempowering and disconnected me from both her and me.

| BELIEFS: REBT (by Albert Ellis, from: *Feeling Good,* by David Burns, 1980) | | |
|---|---|---|
| | **BELIEF** | **WHAT IT LOOKS LIKE** |
| ☐ | **ALL-OR-NOTHING THINKING** | You see things in black-and-white categories. If your performance falls short of perfect, you see yourself as a total failure. |
| ☐ | **OVERGENERALISATION** | You see a single negative event as a never-ending pattern of defeat. |
| ☐ | **MENTAL FILTER** | You pick out a single negative detail and dwell on it exclusively so that your vision of all reality becomes darkened, like the drop of ink that discolours the entire beaker of water. |
| ☐ | **DISQUALIFYING THE POSITIVE** | You reject positive experiences by insisting they *"don't count"* for some reason or other. In this way you can maintain a negative belief that is contradicted by your everyday experiences. |
| ☐ | **JUMPING TO CONCLUSIONS** | You make a negative interpretation even though there are no definite facts that convincingly support your conclusion. |
| ☐ | **MIND READING** | You arbitrarily conclude that |

| | | |
|---|---|---|
| | | someone is reacting negatively to you, and you don't bother to check this out. |
| ☐ | **THE FORTUNE TELLER ERROR** | You anticipate that things will turn out badly, and you feel convinced that your prediction is an already-established fact. |
| ☐ | **MAGNIFICATION (CATASTROPHISING) OR MINIMISATION** | You exaggerate the importance of things (such as your goof-up or someone else's achievement), or you inappropriately shrink things until they appear tiny (your own desirable qualities or the other person's imperfections). This is also called the *"binocular trick."* |
| ☐ | **EMOTIONAL REASONING** | You assume that your negative emotions necessarily reflect the way things really are: *"I feel it, therefore it must be true."* |
| ☐ | **SHOULD STATEMENTS** | You try to motivate yourself with "should," and "shouldn't", as if you had to be whipped and punished before you could be expected to do anything. "Musts," and "oughts," are also offenders. The emotional consequence is guilt. When you direct a "should" statement toward others, you feel anger, frustration, and resentment. |
| ☐ | **LABELLING AND MISLABELLING** | This is an extreme form of overgeneralisation. Instead of describing your error, you attach a negative label to yourself: *"I'm a loser."* When someone else's behaviour rubs you the wrong way, you attach a negative label to them: |

| | | |
|---|---|---|
| | | *"He's a #! @*&% louse."* Mislabelling involves describing an event with language that is highly coloured and emotionally loaded. |
| □ | **PERSONALISATION** | You see yourself as the cause of some negative external event which in fact you were not primarily responsible for. |

*Table 2.* REBT Beliefs

## Elliott Revisited: Understanding The Cognitive Distortions

Let's go back to Elliott. His three different emotional responses can be unpacked through the lens of REBT:

- **Depression:** Driven by *Emotional Reasoning, "I feel worthless, so I must be."* His emotions distort reality, feeding the belief that he is fundamentally unlovable.
- **Anger:** Rooted in *Mislabelling,* he sees his wife not just as someone making a choice, but as an ungrateful betrayer, fuelling his fury.
- **Relief:** Possibly linked to *Mind Reading,* he assumes she was a problem to begin with, and that her departure is purely beneficial, without understanding her perspective.

Identifying these distortions is the first step toward healing. But the second step, restructuring those beliefs, is the harder work. And it *is* work.

As Ellis pointed out:

1. If irrational beliefs, not events, cause distress, we will stay stuck if we cling to them.
2. The more we rehearse them, the more power they gain.
3. Healing requires rewiring those beliefs, painstakingly,

intentionally, and repeatedly.

## Closing Thoughts

The mind is both a battlefield and a sacred space, a place where distorted beliefs can take root, but also where truth can be planted and nurtured. Cognitive psychology and Scripture together offer a framework for recognizing and reshaping the patterns that shape our lives. But awareness alone is not enough. Healing takes more than insight; it requires courage. When we dare to face what wounded us, when we find the strength to name the toxins we've carried, and when we receive the grace to believe what is true, their power to define us begins to loosen.

In the next chapter, we'll take a closer look at the specific mental toxins that keep us stuck, thoughts shaped by fear, shame, perfectionism, and self-judgment. These aren't just abstract ideas; they are deeply personal, often tied to wounds we've carried for years. But identifying them is the first step toward healing.

This is not about blame. It's about freedom. Because when we begin to see these toxic patterns for what they are, lies that have entangled our minds and hardened our hearts, we can begin to loosen their grip. And in their place, we can receive something far more life-giving: the mind of Christ, renewing us from the inside out.

---

## Declarations

I declare that my mind is no longer ruled by fear, shame, or old patterns of distortion—I am governed by the Spirit, and His peace anchors me.

I declare that the lies I once believed no longer have authority over me. God's truth is renewing me daily, rewiring my thoughts and realigning my heart.

I declare that I am not a prisoner of my past. What was not transformed in me before is now being healed by the love of God, and I will not pass on what He is redeeming.

I declare that I have the mind of Christ. I see myself, others, and the world through the lens of grace, not judgment. My thoughts are becoming whole, and my life is being made new.

---

## Prayer

*Loving Father,*
*You know the hidden places in my mind, the thoughts I try to manage, the fears I try to hide, the lies I've unknowingly believed. You see the anxious loops I spin, the mental weight I carry, the judgments I cling to. I bring them all to You now.*

*Renew my mind, Lord.*

*Break the grip of falsehood and flood me with Your truth. Replace worry with trust, shame with grace, self-loathing with love. Teach me to think with Your thoughts, to see with Your eyes, and to choose the mind of Christ in all things.*

*Holy Spirit, breathe through the rooms of my mind. Cleanse what is toxic. Illuminate what is true. Teach me how to love You with all my mind, and to rest in the freedom You long to give. In Jesus' name, Amen.*

---

## Reflection Questions

1. Which theory are you drawn to and why?
2. How do the theories discussed in this chapter help you understand the workings of your mind, particularly

in relation to how your beliefs and thought patterns shape your emotional and psychological well-being?

3. In what ways has your body carried the burden of your thoughts? How might greater emotional honesty lead to deeper healing?
4. What is one truth from Scripture you can meditate on this week to renew your mind?

---

## Journal Prompt

Write or draw a short prayer or reflection: What toxic thought, or belief am I being invited to surrender today, so that it can be replaced by the truth of who God says I am? Let your pen move without censoring. See what flows out.

# CHAPTER 7

## *What Kept Me Stuck*

---

> *"The best cure for the body is a quiet mind." ~ Napoleon Bonaparte*
>
> *"The mind governed by the flesh is death, but the mind governed by the Spirit is life and peace." ~ Romans 8:6*

---

### The Mind Under Siege

There's a striking similarity between the mind's dysfunction and physical illness. Physical pathology occurs when foreign toxins like COVID-19 or cancer invade the body. Healing can't begin until those toxins are removed. Likewise, the mind can be poisoned by toxic judgments and assumptions, distorted beliefs that give rise to toxic emotions like shame, guilt, anxiety, negativity, depression, bitterness, and self-loathing. To love God and others with all my mind, I must recognise and remove these toxins. Healing means replacing the mind's lies with God's truth.

In the Sermon on the Mount, Jesus uses the Greek word *merimnao* five times. It means *"to divide"* or *"to pull apart"* (Bauer et al. 2000). What is He warning us about? The kind of anxious worry that tears us in different directions. When I hear myself saying things like, *"She's beside herself with worry,"* or *"I'm going out of my mind,"* I realise I'm echoing something ancient. The old English word for *worry*, *wirien*, comes from West Germanic roots and means *"to slay or injure by biting and shaking the throat"* (Harper, n.d.).

That image stays with me. Worry and anxiety often feel like that, like a wild animal shaking me senseless, sinking its teeth into my mind. And with my lifelong tendency toward hypervigilance, I know what it's like to be held hostage by anxious thoughts. They squeeze the life out of me. My mind becomes divided, and my body bears the cost.

But God never intended for His people to live strangled by anxiety. I know, deep down, that worry is not just draining; it's a kind of unbelief. An addiction. When negative, fearful thoughts come knocking, I'm learning to counter them with God's truth. The Bible doesn't ask me to manage my anxiety. It invites me to let Jesus carry it. To let go. To trust the One who holds me. His therapy is simple but profound: *"Cast all your worries upon Him, because He cares for you"* (1 Peter 5:7).

I'm learning what that means, to worry about nothing and pray about everything. But first, let's explore the mental toxins that hold us back and what makes change so tough.

## The Mental Crusher: Why Change Is So Hard

Years ago, I came across a visual metaphor called *The Mental Crusher* (Vivyan, 2009) (see Figure 3. *The Mental Crusher*). It perfectly captured how our minds resist new perspectives. Essentially, we have a mental "filter" that only lets in information that confirms our current beliefs. Everything else gets squashed, distorted, or ignored, crushed so it no longer challenges the status quo.

This framework helped me understand why my beliefs were so stubborn. Why, even when others offered me love, grace, or truth, I often couldn't receive it. It didn't fit the story I'd told myself for so long.

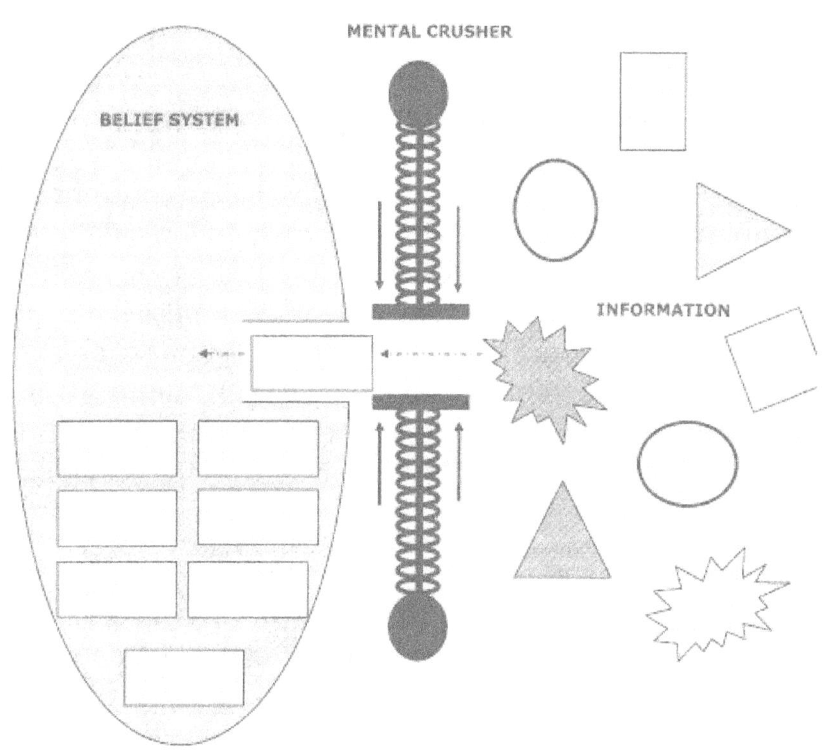


Figure 3. *The Mental Crusher*

## A Biblical Example: The Crippled Woman and the Crushing of Compassion

A vivid biblical example of The Mental Crusher appears in Luke 13. Jesus heals a woman who had been crippled for eighteen years, but instead of rejoicing, the synagogue leader is indignant. Why? Because Jesus healed on the Sabbath.

Their beliefs, rigid, rule-bound, and self-righteous, had so hardened their hearts that they couldn't see the miracle. Their *"mental crushers"* were fully operational, filtering out grace in favour of legalism. Jesus calls them what they are: hypocrites. I've seen this in myself too.

## Dismantling My Own Mental Crusher

For God to heal the wounds in my mind, I've had to confront the distorted image of Him that I absorbed early in life. My father was distant but kind. His absence left me feeling abandoned, like no one would ever come for my heart. My mother, on the other hand, was verbally harsh and rejecting. Her unpredictability taught me that standing up to her would lead to annihilation. From those formative experiences, I internalized a vision of God as distant, silent, and punitive. I believed He expected obedience, but no matter how hard I tried, it was never enough.

That mental framework, the God of my childhood, was deeply embedded. And it crushed any alternative view. A good, loving, pursuing God? That simply didn't fit. But transformation began when I allowed God to tear down those old bricks in my Mental Crusher, those false constructs and show me His true character.

## When Images Are Transferred, Not Transformed

As parents, we are meant to be image-bearers of God to our children. Whether we realize it or not, our children form their earliest impressions of God through us. If we don't allow those broken images to be healed, we risk passing them on.

I see this clearly now. I handed down my image of a distant, unapproachable God to my own children. Not because I wanted to, but because I hadn't yet been transformed. As the saying goes, *what is not transformed is transferred.*

## Renewing The Mind: Beyond Head Knowledge

Healing our image of God requires more than just cognitive

insight. It's not just a matter of learning new information, it's about allowing the Spirit to reshape our deepest orientations: our trust structures, our false selves, and the inner barriers that keep us from surrender.

As Ruth Haley Barton (2011) writes, we can *make space* for this transformation, but we can't manufacture it. We must choose it. And keep choosing it. Daily. Because real healing isn't about *knowing* the truth. It's about allowing the truth to *know* us, until it sinks deep enough to free us.

## Jim's Story

Jim is a small business owner, deeply respected by his clients and colleagues. People admire his sense of responsibility, his intellect, and creativity. But beneath the surface, Jim is addicted to work, though he would never describe it that way. He benefits from it. His constant busyness allows him to avoid the more painful parts of life, like the growing emotional distance with his wife and teenage children. It's easier to stay focused on work than to face the discomfort of their discontent.

Jim's mind is subtly shaped by denial. He chooses not to see the long-term cost of his avoidance. And his spiritual life reflects this. He has little interest in knowing God, seeking Him, or asking what God might want for his life. Paul speaks directly to this in Ephesians 4:22, reminding us that in our natural state, our minds are *"corrupted by deceitful desires."*

## Kyle's Story

Kyle, a friend of mine and a senior executive, is also in his mid-forties. Like Jim, he's addicted to his work, though he doesn't acknowledge it. His clients love his innovation. But outside of work, things are falling apart. He uses pornography as a coping mechanism and is entangled in an emotional affair with a colleague. These behaviours help him avoid the painful truth of his failing marriage and his distant, rebellious daughter.

Kyle's mind, like Jim's, has become captive to false promises. The Message paraphrase of Ephesians 4:17-18 captures this descent:

> *"And so I insist - and God backs me up on this - that there be no going along with the crowd, the empty-headed, mindless crowd. They've refused for so long to deal with God that they've lost touch not only with God but with reality itself. They can't think straight anymore. Feeling no pain, they let themselves go in sexual obsession, addicted to every sort of perversion."*

Both Jim and Kyle are experiencing a breakdown between mind and heart. Their bodies are also carrying the burden. Research shows that emotional signals from the heart to the brain trigger the release of chemicals in the body. The negative emotions they feel, anger, resentment, guilt, envy, are perceived by the brain as stress. That stress activates a cascade of cortisol and adrenaline, energising them to survive, not thrive. But over time, this takes a toll. This wear and tear is sometimes called *accelerated dying*.

But the opposite is also true. When they feel genuine joy, delight in their children, deep gratitude, or positive emotions, they activate an entirely different physiological response. Love, awe, hope, and inspiration reduce stress hormones, support the immune system, and help the body heal. The mind is incredibly powerful.

## Transforming The Mind

God is deeply invested in the healing and transformation of our minds. Romans 12:1-2 urges us, "*Do not conform to the pattern of this world but be transformed by the renewing of your mind...*" The word "*transformed*" is used only one other time in the Gospels, to describe Jesus on the mount of transfiguration (Matthew 17:2; Mark 9:2). This isn't surface-level change. It's radiant, Spirit-empowered transformation.

I'm learning that renewing my mind isn't about willpower. It's about surrender. It's about allowing the Holy Spirit to untangle the toxic lies I've believed and replace them with God's thoughts, His ways, His truth. Ephesians 4:24 describes this renewal beautifully:

> *"...an entirely new way of life, a God-fashioned life, a life renewed from the inside and working itself into your conduct as God accurately reproduces his character in you."*

That kind of transformation requires intention. It means identifying the mental crushers, the rigid beliefs, the harsh inner voices, and dismantling them. And then feeding my mind a healthier diet. Philippians 4:8-9 gives me that menu:

> *"...filling your minds and meditating on things true, noble, reputable, authentic, compelling, gracious—the best, not the worst; the beautiful, not the ugly; things to praise, not things to curse."*

This is not a passive process. It requires constant surrender, especially for someone like me, who has spent years rehearsing worst-case scenarios and catastrophes. But as I open myself to God's renewing work, my mind slowly begins to reflect His peace and truth.

## The Battle For The Mind

The renewal of the mind is a Spirit-led process but make no mistake: it is also a battleground. Satan fights hard for our thoughts. He aims to twist them, poison them, and use them to separate us from God and from others. If we don't actively pursue transformation, we risk losing everything that truly matters.

Both Jim and Kyle once dreamed of making a difference in the world. As young boys, they were bright and full of potential. But they also grew up feeling disadvantaged. Their families couldn't afford the trendy clothes other kids wore. They knew what it was like to feel excluded. By their early twenties, they'd quietly set aside God's kingdom in pursuit of financial success. But now, their minds whisper lies: *You'll never have enough. You are not enough.* And they keep chasing, never satisfied.

A thousand years ago, an unknown monk penned these words:

> *"I wanted to change the world, but I found it was too difficult, so I tried to change my nation. When I couldn't change the nation, I focused on my town. When that failed, I turned to my family. Now, in old age, I realise the only thing I can change is myself. And if I had changed myself long ago, I could have changed my family, my town, my nation, and perhaps even the world."*

Unless Jim and Kyle face the truth, their stories may end this way. But the good news is, it's not too late. It never is. God promises that transformation is possible. Romans 12:1-2 stands as an invitation: surrender your mind, let it be renewed, and discover the fullness of God's will.

## Closing Thoughts

As the mind begins to heal, as truth begins to displace the lies and distortions we've lived with, something deeper begins to stir. Beneath our thoughts lie our wounds, unseen, often unspoken, but profoundly powerful. These are not just mental patterns; they are soul imprints, etched into the deepest places of our being by trauma, loss, and unmet longing. If the mind is where the battle begins, the soul is where the ache lingers.

Healing soul wounds requires more than cognitive reframing or theological insight. It calls for a descent into the tender, sacred spaces where identity has been fractured, where trust has been broken, and where we've questioned not just who we are, but whether we are truly lovable.

In the next chapter, we'll journey into these hidden places. Not to retraumatize, but to bring light. Not to diagnose, but to listen. Because when we invite God into our soul wounds, we discover that He has already been there, waiting, weeping, and ready to restore.

---

## Declarations

I declare that God has not given me the spirit of fear; but of power, and of love, and of a sound mind (2 Timothy 1:7). I declare that I have the mind of Christ (1 Corinthians 2:16).

I declare that imaginations are cast down, and every high thing that exalts itself against the knowledge of God, and I bring into captivity every thought to the obedience of Christ (2 Corinthians 10:5).

I declare that the light of God shines upon my mind and there is no darkness, shadow, or confusion there (Isaiah 50:4; Job 29:3).

I declare my mind open to the hidden things of God, secret things, mysterious things, heavenly things, spiritual things, eternal things, powerful things, precious things, wonderful things, righteous things, elevated things, and profound mysteries of God.

I declare that God keeps my mind in perfect peace (Isaiah 26:3) when it is stayed on Him.

---

## Prayer

*Father God, I repent that I have not discerned harmful and negative thinking, and it has tossed me to and frow. I have not understood that it is about spiritual forces, and I repent for not recognising this. I forgive those in my life who have joined with me in negativity that has affected me, and I release them now.*

*Father God, I repent for the ways I have misrepresented Jesus by my faulty thinking. I invite you to increase my discernment, to increase my discerning of good and evil. I hand you, my fear; I hand you, my negativity. Please break it off me now, in Jesus' name. Father God, I hand You my spirit of negativity and my feelings of defencelessness. I wait to receive what you have for me.*

*Father God, would you come to that place of negative self-talk that is encoded in my amygdala, that erodes my peace and that you would break off the ability for my brain to receive that negativity as a valid thought. Father God, I ask that you supernaturally right now touch my ears so that my ears cannot hear that negative self-talk, and if it comes, please make it indecipherable to me in the name of Jesus. I now receive from you, your presence and protection. Father God, when negativity and hopelessness comes, let me release hope. Let it now be a choice. When despair and sorrow come, let us release life. Thank You, Father God, in your name and authority I pray.*
(Adapted from *Shifting Atmospheres*, by Dawna De Silva, 2017).

---

## Reflection Questions

1. What beliefs about yourself or God have you carried since childhood that may need re-examining?

2. Where might these beliefs be distorting your relationship with Him or others?

3. Can you identify any 'mental crushers' at work in your thinking right now?

4. How do these filters distort love, grace, or truth in your daily life?

5. When do you notice your thoughts becoming anxious, critical, or fear-driven?
6. What would it look like to invite God into that moment instead of managing it on your own?
7. What are some truths from Scripture that speak directly to the lies your mind tends to believe?
8. How could you begin to "feed" your mind with those truths intentionally?
9. Where do you see the Spirit already at work in the renewal of your mind?
10. What shifts have you noticed, no matter how small, that point to healing?

---

## Journal Prompt

Write or draw a short prayer or reflection: Lord, what are the thoughts I keep rehearsing that no longer serve You or me? Let your pen move without censoring. See what flows out.

# CHAPTER 8

## *Healing My Soul Wounds*

---

*"You have to keep breaking your heart until it opens." ~ Rumi*

*"And he departed from our sight that we might return to our heart, and there find Him." ~ St Augustine*

*"Praise the Lord, my soul, and forget not all his benefits - who forgives all your sins and heals all your diseases." ~ Psalm 103:2-3*

---

### When Trauma Touches The Soul

There is a deep ache that trauma leaves behind not just in our memories or nervous systems, but in our souls. It seeps into the very core of who we are, distorting our identity, disrupting our sense of belonging, and often leaving us wondering whether we are truly lovable, safe, or seen. The soul carries our deepest longings, for connection, for purpose, for intimacy with God and others. When trauma disrupts these longings, we don't just feel broken, we feel lost.

In this chapter, I explore what soul wounds are, how they form, how they impact our relationship with God and others, and how healing comes through love, presence, and the Spirit of sonship.

## What Are Soul Wounds?

Soul wounds are the invisible injuries left by experiences that shake our sense of self, belonging, and worth. They are more than psychological trauma; they are ruptures in our capacity to receive and give love freely. These wounds whisper that we are unworthy, alone, or too damaged to be healed.

We may carry these soul wounds from childhood neglect, betrayal by someone we trusted, the loss of a loved one, or witnessing horrors that no one should ever see. For those who live and work in war zones, as I have, these soul wounds are not abstract. They are heartbreakingly real.

## My Own Soul Wound

Like most school days, my packed lunch contained two slices of white bread filled with a pork and ham mixture I loathed. One day I forgot to throw it in the school bin, as I usually did. Knowing my mother would check my schoolbag, I panicked and tossed it from my bedroom window, over the back fence into the park behind our house. How she found it, I'll never know. But find it she did, and the interrogation began.

Fearful of her annihilating rage, I lied. I said it wasn't mine. Unmoved, she reached for the waxed paper dispenser, slowly lining up the serrated edge as she prepared for punishment. The focus shifted from the discarded sandwich to the lie I had told. After a severe thrashing that only silenced me further, she began hurling words, cutting, shaming, unforgettable. I froze, mute in my fear.

Realising I was shrinking into myself, she escalated. She dragged me up the street in full view of our neighbours, declaring how depraved I was and announcing that she was taking me to the police to have me locked away. I broke. Out of sheer terror, I

confessed.
I was eight. There were no defences. I was left isolated, powerless, and confused. What began as a simple need to say, *"I hate my lunch,"* became an unbearable trauma. Food became fused with shame. In adolescence and early adulthood, I struggled to eat in front of others. I couldn't join friends at restaurants or social gatherings. The traumatic memory had sunk beneath the surface, ungrieved and unprocessed, a soul wound.

## The Frozen Child

Children are completely at the mercy of the adults in their lives. I remember shutting down to survive my mother's abuse, trying to stay quiet enough, still enough, small enough to avoid worse. I felt hopelessly rejected and came to believe that the world was as cruel and cold as she was.

Children are completely at the mercy of the adults in their lives. I remember shutting down to keep my mother's abuse from being worse than it was going to be. I felt hopelessly rejected and believed the world was as cruel and cold as her. That belief followed me into adulthood, where I struggled with closeness and confused connection with threat.

In high-stress moments, I freeze, like a deer in headlights. I cannot flee. I cannot fight. I am just... stuck. My body learned that silence and collapse might keep me safe.

I later discovered that this pattern aligns with what trauma specialists identify as the "freeze" response, a hallmark of Complex PTSD (CPTSD). In cases of chronic relational trauma, the freeze response becomes a survival strategy. For years, I withdrew. I lived in my imagination, daydreaming my way out of pain, convinced I was safest disconnected from people.

The threat of being hurt, intimidated, or abandoned was too great. Even today, aggressive or controlling people trigger alarm bells deep within me. I retreat into self-protection, convinced love is an illusion. Everything must be earned. I take refuge in perfectionism and self-reliance, living in a kind of quiet exile.

## The Lie That We Are Alone

The greatest lie trauma tells us is that we are alone in our pain. It isolates us, convincing us that no one, perhaps not even God, can meet us in the depth of our anguish. But throughout Scripture, we see another story: a God who draws near to the brokenhearted (Psalm 34:18), who binds up wounds, and who enters our suffering, not from a distance, but from within.

The soul does not heal through effort or striving. It heals through love. And love always begins with presence. The healing of soul wounds begins not with doing, but with being, being seen, being held, being known.

And yet...

Even in our retreat, God remains near. Soul wounds do not disqualify us from love. They are the very places where God longs to meet us, with gentleness, with truth, with healing presence. To understand why the lie of aloneness is so powerful, we must consider how the soul experiences and processes pain, through emotion.

## The Seat Of Emotions

The soul is the seat of what we call emotions. It is the part of us that feels - joy and sorrow, longing and fear, delight and despair. And this, too, reflects the image of God in us. God has emotions. He is not a distant, cold force but One who feels deeply. Exodus 34:6 describes Him as *"a God of mercy and grace, endlessly patient, so much love, so deeply true, loyal in love for a thousand generations, forgiving iniquity, rebellion, and sin."* Jesus, God in the flesh, wept (John 11:35). He had compassion on the crowds (Matthew 9:36). He felt grief, love, anguish, joy. So do we. To be made in God's image is to be created with the capacity to feel deeply. If the soul holds our emotions, then it follows that soul wounds are emotional wounds.

To love God with all our soul is to offer our deepest selves to Him, our desires, our affections, our very being. It's a call to wholehearted devotion, to living from the core of who we are. But this is no easy thing when the soul is wounded. Emotional injuries, especially those that come early or are repeated over time, can shape our sense of self. We may come to see ourselves as broken, worthless, unlovable, or even superior and disconnected. These distorted identities, born out of pain, block our ability to receive love and live freely.

Whereas mind wounds are mostly intrapersonal (within us), soul wounds are interpersonal, they occur between us. They often result from relational violations: childhood abuse, betrayal, rejection, emotional neglect, manipulation, or abandonment. Sometimes, they are communicated through actions; other times, through the subtle undertow of silence, withdrawal, or words that slice deep. These wounds often go underground, buried beneath our day-to-day functioning, but they fester. They can wreak havoc on our physical health, mental wellbeing, and spiritual life.

Soul wounds don't stay isolated to the past. They leak into the present. Depression, anxiety, addiction, and other mental health challenges can often be traced back to unresolved emotional pain. These wounds can sabotage our relationships, erode our confidence, and make it hard to find purpose. In the end, they can destroy what we hold most dear.

The psalmist knew this kind of agony. In Psalm 7:2–3, David cries, *"LORD my God, in you I trusted; save me; rescue me from all who pursue me, lest someone maul me like a lion, tear my soul apart with no one to deliver."* Soul wounds feel like that, being torn apart from the inside, with no one to rescue us.

And like physical wounds, soul wounds can become infected.

They begin to ooze emotions we don't always recognise as symptoms of deeper pain, resentment, rage, unforgiveness, sulking, bitterness, isolation, emotional exhaustion, anxiety, even despair. We withdraw, lash out, numb ourselves, or live on edge. Eventually, these wounds can split us apart from ourselves, from others, and from the God who longs to heal us.

## The Impact Of Soul Wounds

Soul wounds leave more than emotional pain; they leave neurological imprints. The brain registers emotional pain in the same region as physical pain. It doesn't distinguish between the two. Whether we're wounded in body or heart, our brain releases the same chemical messengers, neurotransmitters and natural pain-relievers, in response. Emotions, then, are not just fleeting feelings; they're physical realities. They rise up in the body. We must learn to understand and regulate them rather than ignore or dismiss them.

### Emotions Are Messengers

Emotions act like internal sensors, detecting either threat or reward, and triggering chemical cascades that prepare us to respond. If the brain detects something life-giving, like a hug from my granddaughter, it releases oxytocin, dopamine, and serotonin, inviting me to savour the moment. But if it detects a threat, like a raised voice or a looming confrontation, it floods my system with cortisol and adrenaline to help me survive.

## Trauma And The Two Brains

Two levels of brain activity are especially relevant when it comes to soul wounds:

1. **The mammalian brain** (fight-or-flight), which protects and activates us in the face of danger.
2. **The reptilian brain** (freeze or collapse), which shuts us

down when fight or flight are no longer options.

A trip to my local pet store helped me see this difference. Puppies and kittens play, tumble, and huddle together for warmth and connection. But lizards? They lie still, unmoving, hidden in corners, disengaged from their surroundings.

This was a mirror of my embedded trauma response. I realized I was more like the lizard. When threatened, I didn't lash out or run, I collapsed. I shut down. I became unreachable. In relationships, this created confusion. My unspoken message was: "Come close, go away." I longed for connection but didn't know how to let it in.

## Branded By Pain

Soul wounds can feel like slavery, like being chained to your own reactions. I felt trapped in cycles of negative thinking, inwardly focused, unable to reach toward God or others. Simone Weil describes this hauntingly: when a person is branded as a slave, it's as if half their soul is taken. *"It's like getting a hot iron branded on your forehead,"* she writes, "like the Romans did to their most hated slaves" (Weil, 1942b, p. 440). The soul becomes marked, not only by suffering, but by the deep, often unspoken belief that the suffering is deserved.

When no answer comes to the question: *Why am I hurting like this?* the soul silently concludes: *It must be my fault.* I must be lazy, indifferent, ignorant, or just bad. The resulting self-contempt crushes the soul. It hardens the heart. Evil, instead of repelling me, settles within me as shame, guilt, and disgust. *"But criminals,"* Weil says, *"don't feel evil in their own hearts. They feel it in the hearts of those they've wounded"* (Weil, 1943a, p. 119).

## The Orphan Spirit

For years, the orphan spirit shaped my inner world. It wasn't something I could simply cast out; it had woven itself into my beliefs and attitudes, shaping how I saw myself, others, and God. I lived as though I had no safe place in God's heart, no sense of being loved, protected, or at home.

Instead, I strove. Everything had to be earned. I was isolated, self-sufficient, constantly hustling for love and belonging. This striving bred anxiety, fear, and frustration (Frost, 2006). I didn't know how to rest. I didn't know how to receive.

## The Invitation Hidden In The Pain

Soul wounds toss us around, pulling us under. But over time, I've come to see that the very wounds I once wanted to erase were actually holding a sacred invitation. They were knocking on the door of my weary, defensive adult self, calling me to turn and embrace the frightened child within, the one who still aches, still rages, still longs to be fully loved.

Healing began when I started answering that door. When I held space for the hard things, not with judgment, but with love. Banishing the orphan spirit took more than head knowledge, it took a personal encounter with God's love. It took a revelation of the spirit of sonship (Frost, 2006). The parts of me that once felt too lost, too orphaned to be found, were finally welcomed home.

And that raises the question: How do we care for our souls?

## Sacred Wounds And Soul Care

This chapter has taken us through the tender terrain of soul wounds, the places of betrayal, abuse, abandonment, and shame that fracture our sense of self and steal our sacred worth. But it has also opened the possibility that, through God's presence and our willingness to listen deeply, even these broken places can become altars of transformation.

I'm still learning. Still opening the door. Still choosing love, toward God, toward myself, toward others. But here's the beautiful truth: soul wounds can become sacred wounds. As Thomas Moore (2016) writes in *Care of the Soul*, when we care for the soul, we become our own therapist. The word *psychotherapy* comes from the Greek *psyche* (soul) and *therapeia* (care) (Harper, n.d.). Soul care is sacred work.

He continues, *"When soul is neglected, it appears symptomatically in obsessions, addictions, violence, and loss of meaning. But when we care for the soul, we engage it in its mysteries, its depth, its darkness and light. We don't try to 'fix' the soul, we listen to it."*

Sacredness doesn't come from the wound itself, but from what happens when we bring our soul's pain into the healing light of love, when we refuse to numb it, bypass it, or silence it, but instead offer it to the One who knows how to hold it.

You are not alone. The path from soul sorrow to soul healing is not linear, but it is holy. May you find the courage to tend gently to your soul, to sit with its ache, and to trust that even in the darkest soil, something sacred is growing.

## Closing Thoughts

Loving God with all our soul means that our identity, purpose, and very existence is rooted in His love. We find true fulfillment not by striving or proving, but by living for His glory and resting in His delight. Yet soul wounds often keep us trapped, looping in self-focus, shame, and distorted thinking. They pull our gaze inward, away from the light, and leave us searching for life in places that only deepen our thirst.

Jesus came to set the oppressed free, not just from external affliction, but from the invisible chains that bind the soul: despair, self-hatred, abandonment, and lies that mask themselves as truth. He came to heal us, body, mind, and soul, and to lead us out of darkness into the wide-open space of love.

We are often unaware of the ways we've become captive to survival strategies, addictions, and counterfeit comforts. We drink from empty wells, hoping to soothe the ache, only to find ourselves depleted. But even there, even in the wasteland, God comes near.

God meets us in the ache, not with striving but with surrender. When we allow ourselves to feel the soul's longing, to bring our pain honestly before God, and to trust that He will not turn away, something sacred begins to grow. The soil of suffering, when watered with grace, becomes fertile ground for transformation.

There is hope. You are not beyond healing. Your soul was made for love, and the One who made you is still near, still calling you home. May you have the courage to open your soul, wounded, tender, beautiful, and let love do its deep, holy work.

And yet, as we open our souls to God's healing touch, we must also face the deeper ache, the longing that persists beneath the surface. This longing is not a flaw to be fixed, but a sacred hunger that speaks to the very heart of who we are. It is the ache for belonging, for love that heals and restores, for a life that feels whole and true. Before these longings can be healed, they must be acknowledged and brought into the light.

In this next chapter, we will linger with this ache, the hunger of the soul that often goes unnoticed, yet calls out to us with a voice that cannot be ignored. It is not a sign of weakness but a divine invitation, a call to embrace our deepest desires and to bring them to the One who understands and holds them. For it is in our longing that God's presence draws near, and through this ache, we begin to discover the fullness of His love.

Let's step into this space together, with open hearts and a willingness to trust that even in our yearning, we are never alone.

## Declarations

I declare healing over my soul wounds and the patterns of negative thinking that have held me captive. I renounce their destructive influence and speak the truth of God's word over them - that I am healed.

I declare that I will no longer act out these wounds or allow them to control me.

I declare that I am slamming the door on the enemy's hold over my pain, refusing to let him have any more access.

I declare forgiveness over those who have wounded me, and forgiveness over myself for continuing the cycle of self-abuse and harm to others.

I declare restoration over my soul, trusting in the promise of Psalm 23.

## Prayer

*Oh, Jesus,*
*You know every one of my soul wounds and sorrows. You know all of my losses, Lord, and you grieve with me. I invite you into all that I am feeling now; I open the door to each of these sorrows and invite you in. Come and be with me here. Grieve with me. Love me here. Lift my heart and soul. For you are my healer, and you understand.*
(Adapted from John Eldridge, n.d., Resilient, One Minute Pause).

## Reflection Questions

1. When did I begin suppressing my authentic self to alleviate the anxiety of a parent or authority figure? How

did I adapt to conceal my inner world?

2. How secure do I feel in my closest relationships to express my true self freely?
3. Am I free to be myself regardless of the company I keep?
4. In what ways do I alter my true self or adopt different behaviours to feel safe and accepted by others?
5. What soul pain demands my attention and healing?
6. Can I express this pain through prayer, writing, or drawing as an offering to God?

---

## Journal Prompt

Write or draw a short prayer or reflection: *What were you trying to protect me from? What would healing look like?* Let your pen move without censoring. See what flows out.

# CHAPTER 9

## *My Soul Laid Bare*

---

> *"And in the end, we were all just humans... drunk on the idea that love, only love, could heal our brokenness" ~ Poindexter, 2015*
>
> *"The Lord is my shepherd, I lack nothing. He makes me lie down in green pastures, he leads me beside quiet waters, he refreshes my soul." ~ Psalm 23:1-3 (MSG)*

---

### Wounds Without Words

The ache of a soul wound is not always easy to name. It can emerge quietly, through longing, disconnection, or a sudden collapse of meaning. This chapter explores the hidden pain we carry deep within, the wounds that go beyond words, and touch the very core of who we are.

When I returned from working with war-traumatized communities, I didn't realize I was carrying a soul wound. For months, I had been immersed in the stories of loss, grief, and resilience. I had walked alongside survivors who had witnessed loved ones slaughtered, children orphaned, and entire villages destroyed. Their pain had become a part of me.

Coming home, I was raw, yearning for rest, connection, and

comfort. But just days after returning, I found myself in a painful interaction with someone I deeply loved. I needed gentleness, but instead, I felt misunderstood and emotionally attacked. The pain of that moment went deeper than I could make sense of at the time. My body shut down. I withdrew emotionally. I couldn't explain why it hurt so much, only that something in me had collapsed.

Looking back, it's clearer now. I was already carrying the weight of so many stories, so much suffering absorbed into my spirit. This moment struck a deeper wound: the fear that I wasn't safe. Not even loved. The fear that I was too much, and at the same time, not enough.

## What Does The Bible Say About Soul Wounds?

In Hebrew, the words *nephesh* or *neshamah* mean *"soul"* or *"breath of life,"* representing the invisible force within that enlivens the body (Brown et al., 2000). The Bible teaches that *"the life [nephesh] of the flesh is in the blood"* (Leviticus 17:11; 3 John 2). The soul and the heart are often used interchangeably (Deuteronomy 6:5; 26:16), but there's a difference between soul and spirit (1 Thessalonians 5:23; Hebrews 4:11-13). The soul seems to encompass the core of the self, our deepest sense of life and personhood.

When Jesus tells us to *"love the Lord your God with all your heart and with all your soul and with all your mind and with all your strength,"* He connects the soul not just to the spirit, but also to the body and mind. A wounded soul requires a holistic approach to healing, including physical, emotional, and spiritual restoration.

Jesus, throughout His earthly ministry, healed people in all these areas. He took on our infirmities, bore our diseases, and in doing so, demonstrated His care for the whole person (Matthew 8:16-17). Acts 10:38 (MSG) captures this wholeness: *"He went through the country helping people and healing everyone who was beaten down by the Devil."*

Jesus' mission was to heal the whole person, to bring freedom to the captives and healing to the wounded. When He encounters pain, He offers not only spiritual healing but physical and emotional restoration as well.

Peter echoes this in 1 Peter 2:25 (MSG), saying, *"His wounds became your healing. You were lost sheep with no idea who you were or where you were going."* This speaks to the deep emotional healing Jesus offers, touching not just the body, but the very wounds of the soul.

## The Tyranny Of The Inmost Being

Scripture often refers to our *"inmost being"* as *koilia*, the deep place where our thoughts, emotions, and choices dwell (Strong, 1995). This is the place Jesus longs to inhabit, where *"rivers of living water"* can flow (John 7:37-38). Imagine Jesus standing at the Feast of Tabernacles, raising His voice above the celebration to plead, *"Come to me if you are thirsty. Drink deeply and be filled".* His appeal wasn't casual, it was urgent, passionate. Why? Because He knows how easily we run dry.

Psalm 51 reminds us that God isn't impressed with sacrifices or performance. What He desires is a broken and contrite heart, an honest, yielded soul. He wants access to the deep places. But so often, we resist. We distract ourselves, deny our pain, and remain distant from the very One who can satisfy our thirst.

If we don't surrender our inmost being to Christ, it can enslave us. Our unfulfilled longings, buried and unrecognized, begin to rule us. This is where addictions, outbursts of anger, and emotional detachment often take root.

In my own story, I had been unaware of the demands I was placing on those closest to me. My thirst for comfort, connection, and understanding, unspoken and unmet, led to withdrawal and disconnection. Perhaps the deepest parts of me had not yet been touched by love, only by pain. And to engage with those longings, to name them and bring them into the light, felt terrifying. Vulnerable. Risky. Too childlike. Too needy.

## How Does Thirst Motivate?

One of the most poignant images in Scripture that speaks to our inmost being is that of thirst. Psalm 42:1 captures it so vividly: *"As the deer pants for streams of water, so my soul pants for you, my God."* The Message brings it closer to the heart with, *"I'm thirsty for God-alive."* This kind of thirst isn't casual, it's desperate. The word *"pants"* evokes the image of a dry-mouthed gazelle, weakened from a long drought, longing for even a trickle of water (Bible Hub, 2024). That same deep ache is echoed in Psalm 119:20: *"My soul is consumed with longing..."*

Imagine being lost in a searing desert, parched, disoriented, your body crying out for water. Then you spot what looks like shimmering water on the horizon, you run toward it, heart pounding, only to discover it's a mirage. That kind of disillusionment is deeply familiar to those of us who have tried to quench our thirst from the wrong wells.

Yet, the invitation is always there, for those who know how truly thirsty they are. God calls out with longing in Isaiah 55:1: *"Come, all you who are thirsty, come to the waters; and you who have no money, come, buy and eat! Come, buy wine and milk without money and without cost!"* It's an extravagant offer, yet it's only received by those who know their desperation.

There was a time when I became achingly aware of my own thirst. I knew I would die unless I found water. It consumed me, this longing for something, anything, to satisfy my soul. But like chasing mirages in the desert, I went after things that only deepened the dryness. I followed paths I thought would lead to life, only to end up emptier than before. Jeremiah 2:13 rang painfully true: *"My people have committed two sins: they have forsaken me, the spring of living water, and have dug their own cisterns, broken cisterns that cannot hold water."* We all do it. I went searching for fullness in all the wrong places. I dug my own wells, chasing after empty promises, instead of coming to the Source of Living Water.

## A Common Struggle

I think of Kyle, how he ran after the recognition of his achievements, measuring his worth by his ability to come through for clients. His wife, in her own thirst, turned to her family, needing her husband and children to meet her emotional longings. And I, too, without even realizing it, placed that same demand on those closest to me, to come through for me, to fill what only God could fill.

The truth is, none of us trusted God to be the One who would provide for our deepest needs as we worshipped Him and served others. We clung to self-reliance, protecting ourselves from the very vulnerability that would lead us back to the Source. And the cost? The very things we were trying to avoid: the loss of God's felt presence… and the loss of our true selves.

Now, as Kyle and his wife approach midlife, they're facing what many do, a sobering recognition that the things they once counted on to make them feel full have left them empty. They're circling around a deep, painful question: *What if all this striving has led me nowhere?* Maybe, just maybe, God is allowing them to come to the end of their own resources. To finally see that the wells they've been digging are cracked and dry. It's a dark place to be, but also a merciful one. Because when what once satisfied no longer does, and the mirages vanish, we're finally able to see the real water.

God is robbed of glory when we refuse to come to Him for life.

We elevate other sources, achievement, relationships, control, affirmation, and shape our lives around them, hoping they'll satisfy. But they never can. What we depend on for satisfaction becomes our god, but only one God can give life.

## Closing Thoughts

To heal soul wounds, we must name the ache, bring our inmost being into the light, and receive the living water Jesus offers. This is not a one-time decision but a posture, a continual turning toward Him, again and again.

It takes courage to feel thirst. It takes surrender to let God touch the places we've tried to hide or numb. But the promise is this: when we come honestly, bringing our raw, broken, aching selves, He will not reject us. His healing runs deep.

This is the way of soul healing: not the path of striving, but of yielding. Not performance, but presence. Not perfection, but intimacy with the One who knows the deepest places of our hearts and still says, *Come.*

He's not just building a cottage. He's making a palace.

Let Him in.

And yet, as we surrender our souls to His healing touch, we must also turn toward the heart and spirit, the deepest places where our wounds may run even deeper. Our hearts, tender and vulnerable, have been shaped by pain, disappointment, and brokenness. Often, our spirits carry scars we may not even fully recognize. These wounds influence how we live, how we love, and how we relate to God and others.

In the next chapter, we'll turn to the heart and spirit, those sacred, hidden places that hold both the treasures and the scars of our lives. God longs to heal those wounds too. His desire is to restore not just our bodies and minds, not just our souls, but our hearts and spirits. For when the heart is healed and the spirit restored, we become fully alive in the love of God.

This is a journey of deep healing, not merely of the body or mind, but of the very core of who we are. Let's take that next step together.

## A Closing Blessing

May the God who sees you in your hidden places gently call you out.

May His presence be your safety, His gaze your comfort, His love your healing.

And may the soul wounds you carry become places where grace flows, not only for you, but for others.

---

## Declarations

I declare that my story matters and my wounds do not disqualify me, they are the very places God is meeting me with His love.

I declare that I am no longer defined by shame, fear, or rejection. I am defined by the One who calls me beloved.

I declare that God is healing the deepest parts of my soul, restoring what was lost, stolen, or broken.

I declare that I am safe to feel, safe to grieve, and safe to hope again, because I am held by a faithful God.

I declare that my life will bear witness to the beauty of redemption. What the enemy meant for harm; God will use for good.

---

## Prayer

*A Prayer for the Wounded Soul*

*Loving Father, You see every part of me; nothing is hidden from Your eyes. You know the wounds I carry, the tears I've cried in silence, the places in me that still ache. You were there when the pain entered. You never left. And now, You gently call me into Your presence to begin again.*

*I come to You not with strength, but with surrender. I bring You the pieces of my soul that feel too broken, too bruised, too burdened. I invite You, Jesus, into the memories I've tried to bury. Into the loneliness I've carried. Into the identity I've questioned. Heal what I cannot heal on my own.*

*Where I have believed lies, speak Your truth. Where I've closed my heart to protect it, teach me how to open it again. Where shame has kept me silent, remind me that I am chosen, cherished, and never beyond redemption.*

*Thank You for being patient with my process, for never rushing me, never condemning me, never walking away. Let Your Spirit breathe new life into the dry and weary places within me. May Your love rewrite the story I've been telling myself.*

*Restore my soul, Lord. Restore what was taken. Rebuild what was shattered. Renew the joy of being fully known and fully loved by You. In the name of Jesus, the Healer of my soul, Amen.*

---

## Reflection Questions

1. Where have you been hiding emotionally or spiritually?
2. Are there soul wounds you've been avoiding, places where you've felt too vulnerable to let God in?
3. What would it look like to respond to His question,

"Where are you?" with honesty and openness?

4. Who can you allow to see your heart, so that healing can begin?

---

## Journal Prompt

Write or draw a short prayer or reflection: How has my wound has shaped my sense of identity, my relationships, and my connection with God? Let your pen move without censoring. See what flows out.

# CHAPTER 10

## *When My Spirit Shatters*

---

> *"The Lord is close to the brokenhearted and saves those who are crushed in spirit." ~ Psalm 34:18*
>
> *"Above all else, guard your heart, for it is the wellspring of life." ~ Psalm 4:23*

---

### When The Heart Breaks

Has your heart ever been broken? In 2022, journalist Eva Wiseman wrote an article in *The Guardian* titled *'Clinically awful': why the pain of a broken heart is real*. One excerpt tells a striking story:

> *"In the winter of 2004, women began arriving at Japanese hospitals complaining of chest pain and shortness of breath. It had been a month since a major earthquake had shaken the country, causing mudslides, injuring thousands, and killing 68. Doctors connected the women to ECG monitors and saw changes similar to those in heart attacks. Yet further tests revealed no blockages. Instead, their hearts had changed shape. Soon, doctors diagnosed the condition as Takotsubo cardiomyopathy, or 'broken heart syndrome'."*

Heartbreak, it turns out, is not just a metaphor. In Japan today, up to 7% of all sudden cardiac hospital admissions are diagnosed as Takotsubo. After a traumatic event, stress hormones can weaken the left ventricle, leaving the heart unable to pump effectively. For a time, it simply gives up. And it hurts.

The condition shows just how profoundly emotional trauma can affect our physical health. Women especially are impacted, with heartbreak triggering inflammation, fragmented sleep, anxiety, depression, cognitive decline, altered gene expression, and even early death (Williams, 2022). Reflecting on her own divorce, Florence Williams writes that *"our cells listen for loneliness,"* and warns that unresolved grief increases risk for long-term illness and premature mortality.

Grief, then, is not only emotional; it is profoundly physical and spiritual. The loss we carry can lead to a sense of desolation, despair, and even spiritual disorientation. Questions about God, faith, and the meaning of suffering often surface. And sometimes, the body itself begins to bear the weight.

But this interconnectedness, between body, mind, and spirit, also points to the possibility of deep healing. Just as grief touches every part of our being, healing can too. When we recognize how our emotional wounds affect our physical and spiritual health, we open the door to holistic restoration.

The mending starts when we invite God into the midst of our grief, trusting that He holds both our broken hearts and our fragile bodies. The path to healing is not simply about managing symptoms, it's about allowing God's presence to restore us at the deepest levels of our being. Even as heartbreak may manifest in the body, there is a spiritual truth underneath: the heart, as Scripture affirms, is the wellspring of life. And God, who knows our hearts, longs to make them whole again.

## The Scriptures On The Heart/Spirit

The heart and spirit are often used interchangeably in the Bible.

Surprisingly, the Bible mentions the heart as the space where thinking occurs, describing it as thinking in our hearts, not our heads, (Matthew 15:19). The Scriptures also tell us that the body without the spirit is dead (James 2:26). Genesis 2:7 mentions the creation of the first man and how Yahweh breathed life into his nostrils. The Hebrew words used here, *ruach* and *neshamah,* and later the Greek word *pneuma* all mean *"breath, wind, or spirit"* (Strong, 1995). Proverbs 4:23 speaks of the heart being the *"wellspring of life,"* translated mostly as from the heart flow the springs of life. The Hebrew literally means that what flows from the heart are the outgoings of life. Picture the heart together with the spirit as a stream that continually flows within to influence our wellbeing and without to those around us.

The Scriptures affirm that God has a heart too, *"I have found David son of Jesse, a man after my own heart"* (Acts 13:22). God is also referred to as spirit recorded in John 4:24 (MSG), *"God is sheer being itself - Spirit. Those who worship him must do it out of their very being, their spirits, their true selves, in adoration."* Our heart/spirit is the breath of God within us shining through the soul. Therefore, to love God with all our heart means that we prioritise Him above all else, allowing His love to shape and guide our attachments, affections, decisions and our inner life in relation to God, or that part that engages with God.

God speaks powerfully to a broken heart/spirit. In Isaiah 61:1-3 (NLT) Jesus said of Himself:

> The Spirit of the Sovereign Lord is upon me,
>   for the Lord has anointed me
>   to bring good news to the poor.
> He has sent me to comfort the brokenhearted
>   and to proclaim that captives will be released
>   and prisoners will be freed.
> He has sent me to tell those who mourn
>   that the time of the Lord's favor has come,
>   and with it, the day of God's anger against their enemies.

> To all who mourn in Israel,
>   he will give a crown of beauty for ashes,
> a joyous blessing instead of mourning,
>   festive praise instead of despair.
> *In their righteousness, they will be like great oaks*
>   *that the Lord has planted for his own glory.*

The expressions *"burdened and battered"* and *"brokenhearted"* are not metaphors like, *"I am the door"* (spoken by Jesus). In Hebrew, the word for *"brokenhearted"* literally means *"shattered or to crush"* (Strong, 1995). In Isaiah 27:11 God uses the same word to describe a dry bush with dry twigs that snap or the breaking of a branch. Isaiah 21:9 uses the same word to describe the idols of Babylon that lie shattered on the ground. Isaiah 38:13 uses it to describe a broken bone. Clearly, the heart can be shattered and broken, literally, and Jesus assumes we all have broken hearts/ spirits:

- **Psalm 34:18**: *"The Lord is close to those whose hearts are broken, and He rescues those whose spirits are crushed."*
- **Psalm 147:3**: *"He heals the brokenhearted and gently bandages their wounds."*
- **Luke 4:18**: *"The Spirit of the Lord is upon me, for He has anointed me to bring good news to the poor. He has sent me to heal the brokenhearted, to free the captives, and to release those held in darkness."*
- **Jeremiah 17:14**: *"Lord, heal me, and I will be healed. Save me, and I will be saved. You are the one I praise."*
- **Psalm 20:20-21 (CEV)**: *"You allowed me to suffer, but You will lift me from this deep pit and give me new life. You will make me great again and take my sorrow away."*
- **Matthew 11:28**: *"Come to Me, all of you who are weary and carrying heavy burdens, and I will give you rest."*
- **Isaiah 43:1-4**: *"Do not be afraid, for I have redeemed you; I have called you by name, you are Mine. When you go through deep waters, I will be with you; and when you go*

> *through rivers, they will not overwhelm you. When you walk through fire, you will not be burned, and the flames will not consume you. For I am the Lord, your God, the Holy One of Israel, your Savior... Because you are precious in My sight and I love you..."*

It's incomprehensible that God doesn't care about healing broken hearts and spirits. If God honours our wounds and tears, we should too. Avoiding it worsens the pain. Healing comes from naming and grieving.

## Stuck Tears

We have seen how untended sorrow affects our body and life-energy. A broken heart/spirit is not something we readily embrace - stuck tears are evidence that one is not strong enough to cry. We hide them because they are dangerous; a man on the run finds that compassion, love, or even tears can be his greatest danger (Courtenay, cited in Fahkry, 2017). Neglected grief keeps his heart pressed down, and lacking joy. That is why the Scriptures are filled with examples of lament and healthy grieving. The ability to put words to our sorrow, to grieve our losses, and engage with God releases the hold that heart/spirit wounds have on our being.

Inner healing does not often come to those who live with stuck tears. My friend Charlotte hides her brokenness from herself and others, especially those in our church. She fears judgement and alienation after her affair that destroyed her marriage. Yet she had no peace and little support. Surprisingly, God's desire for Charlotte is to embrace her broken heart. *"What you're after is truth from the inside out. Enter me, then; conceive a new, true life"* (Psalm 51:6 MSG). If Charlotte is not strong enough to cry, change will be blocked. She once said to my husband, *"I cannot undo the past or what was done. And I cannot avoid the ultimate futility - death, so I may as well end my life now."* Her stuck tears resulted in a sense of meaninglessness (Neufeld, 2010).

Stuck tears can also lead to burnout and/or aggression. Sexually abused as a five-year old, my client Michael stuffs his responses so far down that as an adult, he is unable to contact them. Michael is scheduled for a court appearance after assaulting a man in a bar. It is his third offence. *"When something is not working for you and you can't feel sadness and disappointment, you go into a foul mood and attack verbally or physically"* (Neufled, 2010).

Michael's un-cried tears not only increase his anxiety, stress, and aggression (Frey, 1985), they move him towards isolation rather than connection (Nelson, 2009). Even though his deep hunger for connection makes him capable of loving and being loved, it also makes him capable of wounding and being wounded. Psalm 34:18 expresses what King David deeply knew in his heart, *"The Lord is close to the brokenhearted and saves those who are crushed in spirit."* Michael must understand that there are many things that can only be seen through eyes that are strong enough to cry.

When Charlotte and Michael are strong enough to cry, when they are no longer defined by their stories, vulnerabilities, or weaknesses, they are free to be present to their true selves and offer their healing presence to the world. Wholehearted freedom could be defined as:

- Given over to God.
- Loving others well.
- Feeling secure in our inner being.
- Freedom from self-protection.
- Freedom from others' expectations.
- Responsiveness to God's Spirit.

Jesus came to set us free.

## Christian Community, Tears, And Brokenness

In the Christian community tears can be considered a sign

of weakness rather than strength. It does not always handle a broken heart/spirit well. Neither did King David's family in the Old Testament. After Tamar was raped by her half-brother Amnon, Absalom abuses her a second time by his flawed counsel, *"Now, my dear sister, let's keep it quiet - a family matter. He is, after all, your brother. Don't take this so hard."* In other words, *"Get over it!"* The result of this advice was, *"Tamar lived in her brother Absalom's home, bitter and desolate"* (2 Samuel 13:20 MSG). Tamar's physical and emotional heart/spirit wounds were minimised, ignored, and left unhealed. Even though David was a man after God's heart, his family was broken.

How often do we hear after a painful loss, *"Don't be sad - your [husband, wife, father, mother, child, dog] is in a better place and their suffering has ended."* In our hearts we know this is true, but sadness honours the lost one, because they are missed. To mourn the loss means they were important to the griever.

There are typically strong messages that decree it is not okay to feel sadness, anger fear or shame. Sometimes in Christian community the mental and emotional heart/spirit wounds people carry are treated in the same fruitless way, negating the Gospel that is designed to set people free.

Despite a tenacious faith that believed God held the answers to my life, I became stuck without a way forward. My church wielded the Scriptures like a scalpel without anaesthetic. My hurt prevented me from taking in the Scripture verses that were thrown like swords. I needed someone to come alongside and gently help me to apply the words to my story.

In John 21, after Peter's soul-destroying betrayal, Jesus does not avoid Peter's pain. Instead, He asks him three times if he loves Him. Could it be that in the repetition of the question, Jesus was healing Peter's hurting heart and calling him to be the man he would eventually become? Could this constitute healing the broken-hearted? Bypassing the pain means we miss the freshness and restoration that comes after the laying down of what is in the way.

Avoiding pain and brokenness blunts the desire for God. Deep down we long for his intimate friendship and the unfolding of the secrets of His kingdom within us. The Holy Spirit longs to walk with us, to speak to our hearts and to heal us.

## What Gets In The Way Of Healing?

Healing is tough, and it's not always a straight path. Often, there are things that can trip us up along the way. You know, we all have our ways of avoiding pain. Sometimes it's a little easier to just push those hard emotions aside, right? Maybe you keep busy, distract yourself, or even dive into something that numbs the pain, like work, social media, or even something like food or alcohol. These can all seem like temporary fixes, but they really don't get to the heart of what's going on.

Distractions might seem harmless at first, but they can keep us from dealing with our hurt. Think about when you're feeling overwhelmed, and you grab your phone to scroll through social media. It's like a quick escape, but deep down, you're still carrying that heaviness, right? And that's where addictions can sneak in too. Whether it is substance use or even something less obvious, like work or shopping, it's all a way to distract from the pain. It's not that these things are inherently bad, we all need breaks, but when they become a way to avoid the emotions we're trying not to feel, they stop us from truly healing.

So, how do we begin to recognize when this is happening? First, it's about paying attention to those moments when we're reaching for something to distract ourselves. Ask, "*Am I avoiding something here?*" or "*What's really going on underneath this?*" Getting honest about it, even if it's just with ourselves, is a big first step toward healing. When we give ourselves permission to face our emotions, rather than hide from them, we open the door for real healing to happen.

## Barry's Story

My husband Barry tells how he hid behind his work because he believed that if he allowed himself to feel his pain and emptiness, he would not be able to handle it. He avoided the possibility of breaking down or never been able to stop crying. Feeling long suppressed emotions *can* feel like dying. When Barry was young, he was overwhelmed when his legitimate emotional needs went unmet. But instead of attributing this to the ineptitude of his caregivers, he blamed the need. The only way to survive was to banish the need, along with the painful feelings of it being unmet.

He lets us in on his story:

> *I embraced my family work ethic, too strongly. I used work to distract from the pain of my internal longings. The steady rhythm of completing a task soothed the disappointment in an incident or a conversation and eventually allowed me tuck away the pain with the other remnants. I could not have told you what was happening in my inner world because my work and functionally nurturing environment kept me safe from the nagging existential questions of worth and acceptance.*
>
> *I followed the pattern of my parent, as they probably did theirs. Somehow the message was clear, to mess with the empty feelings within would be to experience being emotionally out of control. The ability to know another deeply was blocked by rationally evaluating their behaviour or ability to function. I felt the need to be known and accepted beyond the barrier of my performance, but it was unmet. I was not truly known and as I matured, I did not know others. Consequently, that is how I saw all rela-*

*tionships. When I felt something, I blamed the need. As an adult the only way to survive was to banish the need along with the painful feelings of it being unmet.*

*Avoidance came at a high cost. I settled for less and lived in a narrow emotional range, avoiding pain but also missing out on joy and excitement. My addiction drained my desire, leaving me unseen and unknown. Denial felt safe but did not foster abundant life. Facing pain is hard, but denial meant never feeling fully alive. I was in my fifties when my son asked, "Dad what have you done with your pain?" My life changed in that moment. I began the journey of reconnecting with my needs.*

## Closing Thoughts

The journey of healing from heart and spirit wounds is not linear, nor is it easy. It requires a willingness to confront pain, to grieve deeply, and to allow God into the places we often try to protect. Our hearts, though fragile, are also resilient, able to be mended by the One who understands our pain more intimately than anyone else.

Take Barry's story, for example. Despite years of being isolated in his pain, Barry's heart began to heal when he chose to surrender to God's transformative love. His journey wasn't immediate, nor was it without setbacks. But over time, as he opened himself to God's presence, his heart began to soften, and the wounds that had seemed irreparable slowly began to mend. Barry's healing was a reminder that God doesn't just soothe surface wounds; He restores us from the inside out, bringing beauty out of ashes and joy in place of mourning. This is the redemptive work of God in our lives, a process that invites us to trust in His goodness, even when the path to healing feels long and uncertain.

As we face the wounds of our hearts and spirits, we are not alone. God is close to the brokenhearted and saves those who are crushed in spirit. He holds us tenderly, reminding us that our pain is never wasted. It becomes a place for His grace to shine through, and for our hearts to be transformed, not just healed but made whole.

Healing takes time. It involves surrender, vulnerability, and the courage to lean into the love of a God who promises to heal and restore. As we embrace the process, we are reminded that, in Christ, we are never beyond hope. His love is deeper, stronger, and more enduring than any wound we carry. With each step of healing, we are invited to love more freely, live more fully, and allow the peace of God to guard our hearts and spirits, now and always.

But even as we experience this deep and beautiful restoration, there are wounds that go beyond the heart or spirit, they can shape the very way we see and relate to God. These are the wounds that come from spiritual abuse, and they can leave scars that affect every area of our lives, from our sense of worth to our ability to trust. In the next chapter, we will explore the profound impact of spiritual abuse, how it distorts our understanding of God, and the healing that is possible when we invite Him to restore our brokenness in these deeply sacred spaces.

The road to healing from spiritual abuse is often long and fraught with complexity, but it is also filled with the promise of God's redemptive love. As we move to the next chapter, let us remember that no wound is beyond His power to heal, and no lie is too entrenched for His truth to set us free.

---

## Declarations

I declare that God's love for me is constant and unshakeable, regardless of my past or the wounds inflicted by others. I am worthy of His love, and He sees me as His beloved child.

I declare that the lies of spiritual abuse will no longer define my relationship with God. His truth is greater than any distortion or hurt I've experienced, and I will embrace His goodness and faithfulness in my life.

I declare that my pain does not determine my identity. My identity is found in Christ, who heals the brokenhearted, and binds up my wounds. I am a new creation, made whole by His grace.

I declare that I can bring all of my hurt, fear, and shame before God, and He will not turn me away. He welcomes my vulnerability and promises to restore and redeem all that has been lost.

I declare that my past does not define my future. I am free to walk in the peace of Christ, unburdened by the weight of spiritual abuse, knowing that God's love and healing are mine to claim, moment by moment.

---

## Prayer

*Heavenly Father,*
*I come before You with a heart that is wounded and in need of Your healing touch. You see the pain, the shame, and the brokenness that I carry. I trust in Your unfailing love and Your ability to restore what has been damaged.*

*Please heal the wounds of my spirit, my heart, and my mind. Replace the lies with Your truth, and the shame with Your grace. Help me to surrender all my pain to You, knowing that You will never reject me.*

*Give me the courage to walk in Your peace, to trust in Your goodness, and to embrace the freedom You offer. Thank You for Your love that never leaves me. I invite You into the deepest places of my soul to bring wholeness and restoration. In Jesus' name. Amen.*

## Reflection Questions

1. When have you felt like your spirit was crushed or your heart shut down?
2. What helped you survive, and what might still need healing?
3. What messages have you come to believe about yourself because of past wounds?
4. Are those messages true in the light of God's love?
5. How do you typically respond to emotional pain, do you numb it, avoid it, control it, or disconnect?
6. What might it look like to bring that pain into God's presence instead?
7. What image of God do you hold in your pain?
8. Is He safe, present, and compassionate, or do other images get in the way?
9. Where might God be inviting you to soften, to grieve, or to risk connection again?

## Journal Prompt

Write or draw a short prayer or reflection: What is one soul wound I carry, and how might God be inviting me to begin healing it with Him? Let your pen move without censoring. See what flows out.

# CHAPTER 11

## *When God Was Used Against Me*

---

*"Your body is a temple, not a daily dumping ground for another person's pain, anger, betrayal, judgment, hypocrisy, denial, games, jealousy or blame. When you are being psychologically, spiritually or emotionally abused by a person, and they don't care how it hurts you, then it is time to leave what is polluting your relationship with God." ~ Shannon L. Alder*

*"Mind control is built on lies and manipulation of attachment needs." ~ Valerie Sinason*

*"The goal is not to tear down the church, but to free you from an imitation of it." ~ Robert G. Callahan II*

---

### Spiritual Abuse And The Loss Of Sacred Trust

Spiritual abuse occurs when religious beliefs or practices are weaponised to manipulate, control, or instil fear. It can take many forms, coercing someone to conform to rigid doctrines, using guilt or shame to enforce obedience, or exploiting a person's faith for another's emotional or spiritual gratification. Often, it targets those who are vulnerable, with an undeveloped or fragile sense of identity, making them easy to mould and harder to resist.

I remember being forced, as a child, to participate in spiritual practices I neither understood nor chose. My mother wielded religiosity like a weapon. It was her tool of control, shaping me not for love of God, but for the fulfilment of her own unmet needs. She made me memorise pages of her handwritten Bible stories to prepare for Sunday School exams (yes, they were real), living vicariously through my success.

My photographic memory helped me top the state, but the experience left me numb. There was no joy, no sense of intimacy with God, only pressure, fear, and a gnawing emptiness. Looking back, I can name it for what it was: spiritual abuse. Faith became performance. Obedience was survival. And God, though I longed for Him, felt distant, eclipsed by the weight of religious control.

## Spiritual Bypassing

A closely related dynamic is spiritual bypassing, which John Welwood (2000) defined as using spiritual ideas and practices to sidestep unresolved emotional issues or painful psychological wounds. It's often subtle, more about checking out than checking in. This pattern offers a kind of counterfeit peace by suppressing pain, disconnecting from emotions, and avoiding inner truth. Many churches, parents, caregivers, and spiritual leaders unintentionally reinforce this form of avoidance, presenting it as spiritual maturity when in fact it stifles growth.

Alan Jones (1989) offers a striking metaphor:

> *"Too much of both religion and therapy has to do with passing on mere information... A mere description of mystery or the numinous doesn't feed the soul any more than the words "filet mignon" satisfy hunger. Many a priest, minister, or counsellor seems to be playing the game of a distributor of menu cards."*

Jones shares the story of a psychiatrist's patient with anorexia nervosa, who would bring bags of doughnuts to therapy, begging him to eat. Obsessed with food, she was unable to consume it herself, a poignant metaphor for spiritual starvation masquerading as spiritual insight. We can preach what we don't live. Teach what we don't believe. Distribute menus without ever eating.

I learned spiritual bypassing early and, without realising it, carried it into my marriage. Ministry became a salve to escape inner pain. It allowed my husband and me to bypass the difficult work of healing old wounds and confronting broken places. For Barry, work quelled his fears of scarcity, providing a sense of security. Logic and emotional detachment became his shields. For me, spending and travel served as distractions from painful feelings and a deep sense of unworthiness. But these unconscious avoidance strategies only deepened our disconnection, from ourselves, from each other, and from God.

Spiritual bypassing can look like strength but is often a mask for pain. We believed we were spiritually mature, but in truth, we were crusading on shaky foundations. It was exhausting, like trying to hold a beach ball underwater. All our energy was spent on keeping pain at bay. What we avoided was what we needed most: a deeper connection with God, each other, and our inner selves.

## The Allure Of Belonging

People are drawn to fundamentalist churches for all kinds of reasons. For my husband, it was the sense of belonging, a tight-knit community where you're known by name and feel part of something bigger. For me, it was the clear moral guidance in a world that often felt chaotic and confusing. These churches offered familiar rituals, and a strong sense of purpose. I understand the appeal; I was drawn to it too.

When life feels uncertain or overwhelming, it's deeply comforting to be part of a group that promises certainty and salvation. There was a strong emphasis on Scripture, on doing the "right" thing, on being set apart from the world. That felt safe, especially for people like me, who've experienced trauma or instability. You know where you stand, and what's expected of you. There's a kind of structure that feels reassuring. But that structure became a cage.

## A Cage In Disguise

Strict doctrines were enforced not just to guide, but to control. Belonging was conditional. Doubts were seen as disobedience. Emotional pain was spiritualised or dismissed. And slowly, often without realising it, people began to hide, suppressing their questions, silencing their stories, and pretending to be fine.

That was when it stopped being community and started becoming coercion. And living inside that system for a long time, it took years to unlearn the fear and rediscover the freedom that Jesus actually came to bring.

## A Flicker Of Honesty

I first began to sense that something wasn't right when my husband and I conducted a small group on leadership. The church presented itself as the gatekeeper of truth, unyielding, certain, absolute. It had all the answers, and if you dared to question them, you were either rebellious or deceived.

I brought a motley display of candles to the group and asked participants to choose one that represented their spiritual lives. There was a range of answers, but one of the deacons chose one that was unlit and explained that he was lifeless and had no sense of the Holy Spirit's power in his life. He was brave. Everyone else was afraid to share.

## Raising Children In The Shadows

More and more I was uneasy, especially for my children. I remember sitting on the wooden pews, my Bible in my lap, feeling a gnawing dissonance between what was preached and what I sensed deep in my spirit. The pastor spoke of grace, but his voice thundered with condemnation. His sermons left little room for questions, doubts, or the complexities of the human heart. Women were to submit, children were to obey, and any emotional pain was to be silenced with more Scripture and stricter obedience. If you were struggling, it was because you weren't spiritual enough.

I learned early how to wear the mask. I followed all the rules, quoted Scripture fluently, and never let my doubts show. I prayed harder, repented more, served more, trying to earn love that was meant to be freely given. But underneath the surface, I was crumbling. I couldn't name it then, but I was experiencing spiritual abuse: my questions were shamed, my emotions dismissed, my identity tied to performance. And worst of all, I was taught that this was God's will.

I remember one Sunday, during a particularly depressing sermon about hell and judgment, I began to feel faint. My heart raced, my hands went numb, and I thought I might pass out. I told the Pastor's wife afterward, and she said it was probably spiritual warfare, that Satan was trying to stop me from hearing the truth. *"You just need to submit to God more,"* she said. *"Don't give the devil a foothold."*

## No Room For Pain

Looking back, I see how deeply spiritual bypassing was embedded in our church culture. Pain was always spiritualized. Depression? A lack of faith. Anxiety? A sign you weren't trusting God. Grief? You should be rejoicing in heaven's gain. There was no room for lament, for honest emotional processing, or for the human journey of healing. Everything painful had to be prayed away.

We later left that church, but it took years to unravel the damage. The voices of the leaders echoed in my head long after I stopped sitting under the sermons. I would read Scripture and flinch, unsure whether I was hearing the voice of God or the voice of spiritual control. It took time, therapy, and the gentle whispers of the Holy Spirit to begin to untangle truth from distortion.

## Meeting The Real Jesus

One day, in prayer, I sensed Jesus sitting beside me. Not preaching. Not correcting. Just sitting in the silence, weeping with me. That was the beginning of healing, when I stopped trying to please a false god of fear and began to encounter the real Jesus: kind, present, and full of grace.

## The Impact Of Spiritual Trauma

Spiritual abuse wounds the soul by silencing the voice, shaming the heart, and isolating the individual from community. The betrayal and loss of belonging are deeply disorienting, especially when inflicted by those who claim to speak for God. It's not just the actions that hurt; it's the twisting of something sacred into something harmful.

I remember the paralysis that came from feeling voiceless. I drifted into emotional inertia, unsure how to choose life for myself. I felt as though life was happening to me, not through me. It was as though my soul had been dimmed. Simone Weil (1942a, p. 456) captured this anguish:

> *"I'm at a loss, and I fear the worst. The thing I hold most dear, the very essence of who I am, could be taken away from me at any moment. Nothing is safe, not even my*

> *goodness or my life itself... The horror of love, loss, and betrayal haunts me."*

And yet, spiritual wounds can become redemptive. They are not good in themselves, but they can be carried into the presence of the Divine and transformed. That's where redemption begins, not in denial, but in acknowledgment and surrender.

## How Do Heart/Mind Wounds Heal?

Jesus' ministry was not just about healing bodies; it was about healing hearts and spirits. Physical blindness often mirrored spiritual blindness. His healings pointed beyond themselves to a greater promise: the full restoration of our being. He came to save us from our sins, not only to forgive, but to restore.

As Paul reminds us, *"We don't yet see things clearly. We're squinting in a fog, peering through a mist... But it won't be long before the weather clears, and the sun shines bright!"* (1 Corinthians 13:12 MSG). That clarity comes through relationship, not information. Love begins to restore what was lost with encountering Jesus. His mission was to *"destroy the devil's work"* (1 John 3:8b), the lies, distortions, and destruction that separate us from God and from ourselves.

In the movie *Tears of the Sun* (2003), Bruce Willis plays a soldier rescuing refugees in war-torn Nigeria. It's a gritty, painful portrayal of redemption. Watching it stirred something in me, this deep longing to be rescued, to collapse into strength not my own, to be seen and rescued. That's what Jesus offers: not a bypass around pain, but rescue through it. Have you ever tried to heal yourself through willpower? I have. It never works. True change comes through surrender, through allowing Jesus to touch our wounds, to destroy the lies, and to speak truth to our hearts.

When we place our trust in Him, we are reborn (John 3:16). *"Anyone united with the Messiah gets a fresh start, is created new...*

*The old life is gone; a new life burgeons!"* (2 Corinthians 5:17 MSG). That's the essence of spiritual healing: not striving but receiving.

## Closing Thoughts

As we allow God into our heart and spirit wounds, we experience the depth of His transformative healing. But this journey is not without its battles. While God's love and grace flood the spaces of our pain, the enemy seeks to bind us with lies that distort our identity and hold us captive in shame. These lies, often whispered so subtly, can take root deep within, shaping how we see ourselves, others, and God.

In the spiritual warfare for our hearts, the enemy doesn't just attack from the outside; he targets the very core of who we are: our identity. This is the war within. The battle over our self-worth and our sense of belonging in God's love. The lies that we come to believe about ourselves, often rooted in past wounds, become the chains that keep us from walking in the fullness of God's freedom.

This is why we must be vigilant. Just as Proverbs 4:23 urges us, *"Watch over your heart with all diligence,"* we must protect our hearts from the lies the enemy seeks to sow. The spiritual life is about more than just healing from past wounds, it's about rejecting the lies that have shaped our beliefs and agreements with the enemy. It's time to break the pact we've unknowingly made with the father of lies and reclaim the truth of who we are in Christ.

As we enter Part 2 and this next chapter, we explore the war within, our shame and the lies that keep us bound, the ones we've believed as truth. And we begin the work of replacing them with the power of God's truth, so we can walk in the fullness of our identity as His beloved.

---

## Declarations

I declare that I am not a victim. Rather, I am chosen, loved, blessed, and gifted.

I declare that good things will come to me and that I have every spiritual blessing in Christ. I declare that You will bind up my wounds.

I declare that I will no longer be oppressed by my heart/spirit wounds, nor will I hide in my pain.

I declare that I am strong enough to cry and I declare that I am healed, in Jesus' Name.

---

## Prayer

*Dear Father, For this reason, I kneel before You, from whom Your whole family in heaven and on earth derives its name. I pray that out of Your glorious riches You may strengthen me with power through Your Spirit in my inner being, so that Christ may dwell in my heart through faith. And I pray that I, being rooted and established in love, may have power, together with all the saints, to grasp how wide and long and high and deep is the love of Christ, and to know this love that surpasses knowledge - that I may be filled to the measure of all the fullness of God.*

*Now to him who is able to do immeasurably more than all I ask or imagine, according to his power that is at work within me, to him be glory in the church and in Christ Jesus throughout all generations, for ever and ever! Amen.* (Adapted from Paul's prayer to the Ephesians 3:14-21)

---

## Reflection Questions

1. Identify and describe any notable heart/spirit injuries you have endured in the past.
2. Describe your profound thirst and sense of longing.
3. What heart/spirit blockages are you experiencing?
4. How did you manage to deal with these wounds and maintain your well-being?
5. How do these wounds influence your interactions with those close to you?

---

## Journal Prompt

Write or draw a short prayer or reflection: What beliefs or experiences from your past feel more like spiritual pressure than true connection with God, and what might healing begin to look like if you brought them into His light? Let your pen move without censoring. See what flows out.

# PART 2

*The War Within: Shame and Identity*

# CHAPTER 12

## *The Devil's Pact: Lies I Agreed To*

---

*"When life-changing experiences come, the major choice we face is whether to walk the pathway of healing or the pathway of continuing pain...Life has a nasty habit of presenting us with forks in our emotional roads...they present us with some hard choices: either we continue as before, or we make changes that are sometimes painful and almost always frightening..." ~ Clinton & Sibcy, 2006, p. 217*

*"The key problem I encounter working with wounded, depressed, and unhappy people is a lack of connection... starting from a disconnection from themselves and then with others." ~ David W. Earle, Love is Not Enough*
*"It was not so much that he was shut out, but that she was trapped inside." ~ Kristen Heitzmann, Secrets*

---

### How Trauma Twists Truth Into Agreement

When faith is used to wound, something deep inside splinters. We may walk away from the experience, but the internal damage doesn't simply vanish. The shame lingers. The fear seeps into our bones. Over time, we begin to adopt false beliefs about ourselves, about God, and about our worth. We make silent agreements with these lies, not because we want to, but because they feel like the only way to survive.

I didn't realize it then, but I had made a pact. A soul-deep agreement with distorted messages that told me I was never enough, always too much, unworthy of love unless I performed, obeyed, or disappeared. These were not just passing thoughts, they became internal scripts, shaping how I saw myself, how I related to others, and how I imagined God.

It's time to name those lies that make up our false self. To uncover the pacts, we made in pain. And to begin, gently, the holy undoing.

## The Hiding Place

Karen Horney's (1950) psychological insights into the formation of the false self, offer a powerful lens through which to understand our inner struggles. According to Horney, the false self is an unconscious strategy developed in response to deep-seated anxiety and inadequacy, often rooted in early experiences of emotional neglect, shame, or unrealistic expectations. When our true feelings or needs were met with rejection or disapproval, we learned to shape ourselves into who we thought we had to be. The false self - became a defence: a carefully constructed mask to gain approval and avoid vulnerability.

We all do this in different ways. Some of us become pleasers, compulsively needing to be liked and keep the peace. Others strive for perfection or power, chasing success or control to buffer against shame. Some withdraw and hide, convinced invisibility is safer than intimacy. Still others spiritualise the false self, believing that if we act godly enough, serve enough, know enough Scripture, or say all the right things, we'll be safe from rejection. But what we're really doing is protecting the wounded parts of us that still feel unworthy or unloved.

## Creating A False Self To Survive Shame

To understand how shame defences take root, we must return to the early experience of unmet needs, not needs distorted by sin, but *legitimate needs rejected or neglected.* Children instinctively shape themselves into someone acceptable to their parents. If only certain parts are welcomed, if nurturing is inconsistent or unavailable, or if the child is not seen and loved in their wholeness, the result is insecurity, a gnawing sense of being unloved, unlovable, and alone. To survive this rejection, the child begins to layer protective strategies over their tender soul.

They adopt well-defined roles: the golden child, scapegoat, rebel, enabler, lost child, masks that serve to shield them from further hurt. These roles become not only coping mechanisms but entire identities, shaping how they see themselves and relate to the world. Those outside the family might see through these roles, but for the child, and often the adult they become, these adaptations feel necessary and invisible. The problem becomes more than sin. It's not just that I shut down in response to pain and need forgiveness. It's that I begin to believe *I am the problem.* My very self is flawed. Unwanted. Shame enters here, not just about what I've done, but about who I am.

In the silent language of attachment, a parent can convey: *"I see you... and I don't like what I see."* The child hears: *You must hide your truest self; it can never be welcomed or enjoyed.* As John Bradshaw (2005) writes, *"Since one's inner self is flawed by shame, the experience of self is painful. To compensate, one develops a false self in order to survive." Donald Capps (1993) describes shame as "a sin against the self."*

The deeper our entanglement with illusion, the image we've crafted to survive, the harder it becomes to pray. Why? Because we are not praying from our true self. Our attachments, whether to people, roles, possessions, or reputation, bind us. Even our giftedness can be sabotaged by shame. We fear being seen. And so, we see only what we want to see and believe only what we can bear, even if it's not true.

## Believing Our Illusions

I remember once in Assisi, Italy, watching two street performers dressed in white, with flowing garments and wings, posing as angels. The male played a harp. Onlookers were captivated, some even falling to their knees in worship. It was just a show, but it didn't matter. People *wanted* to believe. It struck me how easily we believe illusions when the truth feels too painful.

As children, the illusion we often cling to is that our parents were safe and loving, even when they weren't. To preserve this illusion, we reject our needs rather than confront the heartbreak of emotional absence. The rejection might have come through seemingly harmless statements like:

- *"Leave me alone, darling. Can't you see I'm busy?"*
- *"Why are you always so needy?"*
- *"Big boys don't want to be held all the time."*
- *"That's sissy stuff."*
- *"Stop crying."*

Each message lodges deeply: *My need for connection is too much. I must not need. I must not feel.*

## A Cascade

To cope, we turn the pain inward and disown our neediness. As Dr. John Townsend (1996) explains, this starts a devastating cascade:

- **Our legitimate needs go unmet** - for love, comfort, and connection.
- **Our soul is wounded** - not just by trauma, but by consistent relational absence.

- **We begin to view our needs as wrong** - believing it's safer to deny them than risk more rejection.
- **We suppress our needs entirely** - pushing away the parts of us that feel too vulnerable.
- **We create false solutions** - developing patterns of performance, hiding, and self-sufficiency.
- **We bear the fruit of disconnection** - anxiety, depression, addiction, isolation. As Jesus says in Luke 6:45, *"The mouth speaks what the heart is full of."*

We adopt neurotic strategies not because we're weak, but because we're trying to survive. Yet what once protected us now imprisons us. Hiding our weaknesses may feel safe, but it sabotages healing. We lose touch with our God-created self.

I know this in my own life. As an adult, I didn't relate to others from my true self, that vulnerable, glorious self, made in God's image. I related from a self I had constructed to survive. I exchanged my soul for the belief that I could make life work on my own. I would not depend on others, not even God. Shame taught me to hide the parts of me that felt unacceptable.

Neuroses, as Karen Horney (1950) defines it, originate in the false self, and they serve as defences against shame. Brené Brown (2012, p. 70) defines shame as *"the intensely painful feeling or experience of believing that we are flawed and therefore unworthy of love and belonging."* Someone once said that neurosis is like clinging to a hot stove, because if we let go, we fear we won't eat. We hold tightly to what hurts us because we believe we cannot survive without it.

## Turning Against Myself

In Horney's terms, I turned against myself to avoid the terror that my real self might be exposed. I internalized the belief that my needs were not just unmet, but *illegitimate.* I silenced those parts of myself to preserve attachment, to lower my parents' anxiety, to make life feel safer. But in doing so, I lost access to my truest self, the one God longs to restore.

When we reject our legitimate needs, we disconnect not only from ourselves but also from the God who created us with those very needs, for connection, comfort, intimacy, and delight. But God does not leave us lost in the roles we've crafted or the shame we carry. He meets us right there, not in the polished image we present, but in the hidden places we've tried to protect.

Integration begins when we stop blaming the need and start listening to it. When we dare to bring our ache, the very part we were told was too much, into the light of God's presence. It is here, in this sacred undoing, that we begin to rediscover our soul's true voice. And it is here that God whispers: *"You are mine. I see you. I want you."*

### The Mask I Wore

I remember, in our early married life, wearing the mask of the competent, caring, unshakeable Christian woman. I had learned early that vulnerability was dangerous. Expressing need often led to disappointment. Asking for help seemed to make others uncomfortable. So, I buried my needs beneath performance.

I worked hard to appear tireless in serving others, even though service wasn't my primary spiritual gifting. I tried to meet expectations. I led Bible studies and mentored women. On the outside, I appeared strong. On the inside, I was exhausted, afraid that if I ever let the mask slip, I would be disqualified from love.

But the truth is, the false self cannot be loved. Only the real self, the one who bleeds and breaks and longs, can receive love. God cannot heal the mask. Jesus wants the person behind it.

Let's now turn to what restoration looks like, how truth dispels illusion, how divine love mends the fractured soul, and how we are invited into a renewed identity that no longer needs to hide.

## The Genesis Narrative And The Birth Of Shame

This impulse to hide is not new. It is as ancient as the fall of humanity. In Genesis 3:7-8, we read the story of Adam and Eve after they eat the forbidden fruit:

> *"Then the eyes of both of them were opened, and they realized they were naked; so they sewed fig leaves together and made coverings for themselves. Then the man and his wife heard the sound of the Lord God as he was walking in the garden... and they hid from the Lord God among the trees."*

Here we see the birth of shame: the first experience of being exposed, vulnerable, and afraid. Their instinct was to cover up and hide, not just from each other but from God. It's the same instinct that drives the construction of the false self. The fig leaves are our attempts to cover our perceived inadequacies, and the hiding represents our fear that if God or others really saw us, naked, broken, and messy, we would be rejected.

Yet what is most striking in this story is not just the human impulse to hide, but God's response. God does not storm into the garden with condemnation. He calls out gently, *"Where are you?"* (Genesis 3:9). It's a relational question, not a legal one. God is seeking communion, not punishment. It's the same question He still asks us today, not because He doesn't know where we are, but because He longs for us to come out of hiding and return to intimacy.

## Rejection Of Legitimate Needs To Manage Shame

Shame is not just a feeling; it's a relational wound. It tells us that we are unworthy of love and belonging. Unlike guilt, which says, *"I did something wrong,"* shame says, *"There is something wrong with me."* When shame goes unaddressed, it drives us into patterns of hiding, pretending, and self-protection.

Karen Horney organized neuroses into patterns of behaviour rooted in universal needs that have been dismissed or disparaged. When our legitimate needs aren't seen or met, we don't forget them, we adapt. We learn to protect ourselves from the pain of that rejection through unconscious strategies of survival. These often form the bedrock of our personality, shaping how we relate to others and ourselves.

My husband, Barry, explains that he has a deep-seated need for closeness and connection that often feels overwhelming and urgent. When these needs aren't met, he becomes anxious and stressed. The intensity of this need is often unrealistic, as if it's the most important thing in his life.

It began in childhood, when his basic needs weren't met. Feeling unloved and unappreciated, he developed strategies to survive his parents' emotional indifference. Over time, these strategies formed a shield of shame, whispering that he wasn't good enough.

As an adult, Barry unconsciously reenacted relational patterns shaped by these early wounds. For example, in the early days of our relationship, he deeply believed I would not be emotionally responsive. Though I never intentionally rejected him, he anticipated rejection anyway. He presented me with a version of an old story, one where his needs would go unmet, and responded by rejecting his own needs before I could.

## Shame Shields

When our legitimate needs are not met, or worse, are shamed, we don't simply forget them. We bury them, disguise them, or try to outrun them. These adaptations become our survival strategies, our *Shame Shields* (Brown & Hartling, 2016). But as helpful as they once were, they eventually become the very walls that separate us from ourselves, others, and God.

As adults, the need for connection is replaced by a need for self-sufficiency and independence. We become fiercely self-reliant, reluctant to ask for help, slow to commit, and resistant to vulnerability. Some adopt a need for perfection and control, always seeking to avoid mistakes or emotional exposure.

Horney proposed that children develop three primary coping strategies to cope with shame and unmet needs. These are:

1. **Moving Away** (withdrawing)
   When faced with parental indifference, some children withdraw into themselves. They hide, silence their needs, and keep secrets. Over time, they learn: *"If I withdraw, nothing and no one can hurt me."*

   Moving away was my chosen Shame Shield. My pact with the devil took the form of an internal vow: *"To need is to be hurt, so I will never need anyone again."* I believed life would work best if I withdrew, physically, emotionally, or both. To others, I appeared calm and competent. But inside, I was collapsing. Painful feelings, distress, and anger were all swallowed, internalised, hidden. I secretly believed my very existence was a burden to others, and so I camouflaged my needs. No one would ever see my suffering or my deep longing to be loved and desired simply for who I am.

2. **Moving Toward** (seeking to appease and please)
   Other children become pleasers. Overwhelmed by fear of abandonment or helplessness, they suppress their frustration and try to win the affection of their caregivers. The underlying belief becomes: *"If I can make you love me, you won't hurt me."*

   In adulthood, this strategy manifests as a need for approval, for affection, and for others to affirm their worth. These individuals may long for a partner who will rescue or complete them. They tend to be undemanding, agreeable, and keep life within narrow borders, anything to avoid being too much.

This was Barry's Shame Shield. Although he appeared emotionally attuned, his silences were protective. He shut down to avoid conflict, stress, or rejection. But his detachment caused damage, to our relationship and to himself. His longing was deep: to be loved and accepted for who he truly was, without having to earn it.

3. **Moving Against** (fighting shame with power and aggression)
   Horney observed that some children develop a third strategy, a form of protest rooted in *"basic hostility."* Rather than suppressing their pain, they fight. Their belief becomes: *"If I have power, no one can hurt me."*

   As adults, this strategy takes the form of a need for dominance, control, or superiority. They may develop contempt for vulnerability and a belief in their own rational powers. This can lead to manipulation, exploitation, or an obsession with recognition and achievement, anything to avoid being seen as weak, ignored, or insignificant.

   Moving against was Mitchell's chosen Shame Shield. Disconnected from his inner world, he survived through aggression. He couldn't tolerate authority and reacted explosively when he felt threatened. Mitchell appeared strong, but lived in isolation, hypervigilant and distrustful. Despite his angry self-protection, his deepest longing, often unacknowledged, was to be seen, understood, and safe with others. But his shame compelled him to reject others before they could reject him.

Even though there are exceptions, we tend to choose careers that reinforce our Shame Shield. In doing so, we gain secondary benefits, approval, admiration, control, and these can make our coping style feel like our identity. Barry's *"moving toward"* strategy worked well in his career as an accountant. People viewed him as reliable, kind, and dependable. But beneath that lay a false pride and a hidden entitlement, an expectation of unconditional approval.

Knowing our primary strategy of disconnection can help us understand why we relate the way we do, and why it's so hard to live in the present. We're not responding to what is; we're reacting to what was. And each strategy deepens our disconnection from our true self, from others, and from God.

As Richard Rohr (2013) notes, when we're not used to sitting with anxiety, uncertainty, or unmet longing, we tend to run. If we can't understand our feelings, we grab onto old explanations that make us feel in control, even if they're not true. The more afraid we are, the more we cling to familiar shields. Each strategy is an attempt to manage shame and protect the vulnerable self.

But these Shame Shields no longer serve us. As Alice Walker (1990) wrote, when we build walls to protect ourselves from pain, we think we're shielding ourselves. But in the end, the wall causes more damage than the pain itself. The pain, if we move through it, will pass. But the wall? It stays. It grows moss. It blocks our access to others, and to our own hearts.

The true author of these strategies is not us; it's the enemy of our souls. Satan whispers his lies into our early wounds, and these lies become our operating systems. He uses them to disconnect us, from God, from others, from our own selves. But there is a better way. We were made for abundant life. And that life begins when we dare to name the strategies we've used to survive and begin to surrender them to the One who came to heal.

## The Faustian Bargain: Trading The Soul For Safety

The story of Faust, popularized by Goethe, gives us another way to think about the false self. Faust, a scholar dissatisfied with life, makes a pact with the devil, exchanging his soul for worldly knowledge, power, and pleasure. In doing so, he hopes to transcend his limitations and avoid pain. But the cost is his soul.

The false self is a kind of Faustian bargain. We trade our authenticity, our soul, for the illusion of safety, significance, or belonging. We sell out our true self to gain control or admiration, but we end up alienated from our own hearts and from God. Like Faust, we discover too late that no amount of worldly success or spiritual performance can satisfy the soul's deepest longing: to be known and loved as we are.

## God's Invitation To Be Known

The Psalmist declares, "*You have searched me, Lord, and you know me… You are familiar with all my ways… Where can I go from your Spirit? Where can I flee from your presence?*" (Psalm 139:1,3,7). This is both terrifying and comforting. God sees everything, and He loves us still. He sees beyond our strategies, our false selves, our fig leaves. He sees the wounds beneath our defences. And He invites us to be known, not to shame us, but to heal us.

Jesus embodies this invitation. In His interactions with the broken, He consistently bypasses masks and addresses the heart. He sees the Samaritan woman's failed relationships and offers her living water. He sees Peter's bravado and restores him after betrayal. He sees the leper's isolation and touches him with compassion. He does not shame us into change; He loves us into transformation.

## From False Self To True Self

The shift is underway when we stop striving to be someone we're not and begin to trust that who we are, our true self, is beloved. This is not a call to self-indulgence or license, but to courageous authenticity. Henri Nouwen (2002 wrote, "*The spiritual life is a journey to the centre, where we meet the God who dwells in our inmost being."*

Letting go of the false self is painful. It feels like losing control. But it is also liberating. As we come out of hiding and allow ourselves to be seen, we begin to discover who we truly are - beloved children of God, formed in His image, wounded yet redeemable.

## Closing Thoughts

We all carry stories shaped in childhood, stories that were written by our longing to belong and our fear of being unloved. When those early needs were dismissed or unmet, we didn't stop needing, we just learned to hide. We found ways to protect ourselves from pain, to shield our tender souls from further harm. Yet in doing so, we buried parts of who we truly are.

The strategies we adopted, whether moving away, moving toward, or moving against others, may have helped us survive, but they cannot help us flourish. While they protected us from pain, they also kept us from love. Over time, the walls we built for safety become prisons. The false self, promises control, but it costs us connection.

Yet beneath every defence mechanism lies a soul still longing to be known, chosen, and loved without condition. The invitation of Jesus is not to try harder or fix ourselves; it's to come out of hiding. It's to lay down the shields that no longer serve us and to allow His love to touch the places we've spent a lifetime protecting. He does not condemn our defences; He understands them. But He calls us beyond them, into the freedom of being known and loved as we truly are.

We were never meant to live behind fig leaves. The hiding, the striving, the performing, these things exhaust the soul. For many of us, these strategies have become so familiar, so ingrained, that we no longer know who we are without them. But here's the good news: our true self is not something we must earn or invent. It is the self that God already sees, already knows, and already loves.

Like Adam and Eve, we may be crouched behind trees of shame. Like Faust, we may have bargained parts of our soul for significance or control. Like Karen Horney's clients, we may have long lived from a false self, crafted in fear. But God does not leave us there. His call is not to condemnation, but to communion. He calls us out of hiding, not to expose us in judgment, but to embrace us in mercy.

The rebuild begins when we stop managing our image and start telling the truth. When we stop striving to be acceptable and start receiving grace. When we stop performing and begin to rest in the One who already sees us, knows us, and calls us His own. The false self must be surrendered, not because it was evil, but because it is no longer needed. There is another way. A truer way. The way of love. The way of return.

This journey is not about reconstructing an image of God based on our desires or needs, but about discovering Him as He truly is: Loving, merciful, and good.

As we move into the next chapter, we'll explore the God we've misunderstood, the One whose love has been obscured by our fears and misconceptions. Healing starts with allowing God to correct our faulty perceptions of Him. When we see Him for who He truly is, a God who invites us out of hiding, calls us to Himself, and loves us beyond measure. It's time to let go of the false images we've held of God and embrace the reality of His unshakable love for us.

---

## Declarations

I declare that I am known and loved by God, not for the masks I wear, but for the true self He created me to be.

I declare that shame no longer has power over me, for I am accepted in Christ, and nothing can separate me from His love.

I declare that God's truth is greater than the lies I've believed about myself, and I choose to walk in the freedom of His healing.

I declare that I am no longer defined by my past wounds, but by the love and grace of God that transforms and redeems me.

I declare that I am a beloved child of God, fearfully and wonderfully made, and I choose to live authentically, without fear of rejection or shame.

---

## Prayer

*Lord, I come before You just as I am, with all my brokenness and burdens. I confess the masks I've worn, the false selves I've created to protect myself from shame and rejection. Thank You for seeing me beyond these facades, seeing my heart, my wounds, and my deepest longings.*

*I invite You into the hidden places within me. Heal the parts of me that feel unworthy or unloved. Remind me of who I am in You: beloved, chosen, and free.*

*Help me to lay down the weight of pretence and embrace the truth of my identity in Christ. Teach me to walk in the freedom You have already purchased for me, to live authentically, and to rest in the security of Your unconditional love.*

*I trust that You are making all things new, and in Your presence, I find my true self.*
*In Jesus' name, Amen.*

---

## Reflection Questions

Take a moment of silence. Sit with the question God asked in Eden: *"Where are you?"* Not physically. Emotionally. Spiritually. What are you hiding? What mask are you wearing?
Imagine yourself in Eden again. You've eaten the fruit. You feel the sting of shame. You're hiding behind a tree, clutching your fig leaves. Then you hear God's voice, not angry, but tender, *"Where are you?"*

Can you step out from behind the tree? Can you let Love see you?

---

## Journal Prompt

Invite the Holy Spirit to gently uncover the places you've hidden behind performance, perfection, or people-pleasing. Journal what He reveals. Then, in simple words, speak honestly to God. No pretence. No polish. Just you.

This kind of prayer and journaling can feel raw. But it is the soil of deep healing. For it is only when we allow ourselves to be seen that we can be truly loved. And it is only in the arms of Love that the false self can finally rest.

# CHAPTER 13

## The God I Couldn't Trust

---

*"Genuine trust involves allowing another to matter and have an impact in our lives. For that reason, many who hate and do battle with God trust Him more deeply than those whose complacent faith permits an abstract and motionless stance before Him. Those who trust God most are those whose faith permits them to risk wrestling with Him over the deepest questions of life. Good hearts are captured in a divine wrestling match; fearful, doubting hearts stay clear of the mat." ~ Dan Allender, The Wounded Heart*

*"More than ever, I now find myself in the hands of God. This is what I have wanted all of my life, from my youth. And this is still what I want. But now there is a difference: the initiative is entirely with God. It is indeed a profound spiritual experience to know and feel myself so totally in the hands of God who has taken hold of me." ~ Pedro Arrupe SJ*

*"I am the Gate. Anyone who goes through me will be cared for, will freely go in and out and find pasture. A thief is only there to steal and kill and destroy. I came so they can have real and eternal life, more and better life than they ever dreamed of." ~ John 10:10*

---

## An Inherited Image Of God

Many of us have inherited an image of God shaped more by human brokenness than divine truth, an image that distorts who He is and how He relates to us. My image of God was shaped early on by my father. A memory captures this well: I am fourteen or fifteen years old. The family is nearly finished eating dinner when my father and older brother start provoking each other. Although this isn't unusual, tonight it escalates. They begin punching each other, and it ends with my brother being smashed into the wall, leaving a gaping hole.

Distressed and overwhelmed, I flee the house, walking the streets aimlessly, unsure of where to go. My father eventually comes looking for me. When he finds me, he pulls up in his car, opens the passenger door, and I reluctantly get in. The air in the car is thick with unspoken emotion, but he says nothing. No explanation. No apology. Just silence. Life resumes as if nothing happened.

Though my father was a likeable man, he was emotionally stunted and weak. Every little girl longs to be fought for, to be cherished, to feel protected. My father failed to provide that for me. He did not shield me from my mother's rage. Avoiding meaningful conversations, he spent long hours fishing, sometimes overnight, his retreat from her constant belligerence. Mostly, he was distant and unavailable. This became a prologue to the image I later formed of my Heavenly Father.

On his deathbed, my father was overcome with regret. He obsessively attempted to initiate divorce proceedings, lamenting his failure to carry through on it years earlier. It was excruciating to witness. After his death, I stumbled upon old letters he had written to my mother during their engagement. They brimmed with hope and spiritual passion. When did that dream die? He passed away a shell of a man, a ghost of the hope-filled young man he once was.

Inevitably, my image of God mirrored my image of my father. God was powerful, but unpredictable, even dangerous. I feared that He could protect me but might choose not to if I displeased Him. I imagined Him with more important things to do than care about me. He didn't have my best interests at heart. Trusting a God like that was nearly impossible. Hope was scarce in my childhood. I concluded I was on my own. No one would come for my heart.

And this distorted image didn't stay neatly in my childhood; it bled into my marriage.

## Our Holiday Exchange

The Sunshine Coast of Queensland is often described as *"beautiful one day, perfect the next."* Barry and I were holidaying there by an inland lake near the beach between facilitating marriage events. But during one of those seemingly perfect days, a terse exchange between us disrupted the peace.

We were three weeks away from flying to Sri Lanka for five weeks of ministry. I was under pressure, juggling the marking of postgraduate student papers and preparing a course on developmental attachment theory. I resented that I couldn't fully enjoy our surroundings. That resentment simmered beneath the surface until I snapped at Barry. It wasn't well received. Now, on top of being overloaded, I felt emotionally disconnected from him. I pushed away the very support I wanted and needed.

Prompted by the Holy Spirit, I began to reflect. I asked God to help me see what I couldn't. I realized I had cast Barry in the same light as my father, believing he had abandoned me, that I wasn't worth protecting, not worth fighting for. It was less painful to push him away first than to risk having the old lie reinforced: *"No one will come for you. You are on your own."*

These lies, forged in childhood, shaped my relational expectations, especially in marriage. But the Spirit whispered: *"I will never leave you nor forsake you... I am with you always."* Suddenly, my eyes opened. I saw the lie for what it was. I asked God's forgiveness for agreeing with it, and asked Barry for his forgiveness, too. As my image of God changes, so do my relationships. A clearer view of God's heart brings transformation.

## The Boy And The Butterfly

There's a story of a boy who finds a butterfly struggling to emerge from its cocoon. Impatient, he breathes on it to speed up the process. The butterfly does emerge, but its wings are crumpled and folded. It cannot fly. The boy, horrified, watches as the butterfly dies in his hand. His intervention had forced it out too soon.

How often am I like that boy, running ahead of God, impatient with His timing, mistrusting His silence? I take things into my own hands, trying to manipulate outcomes because I struggle to trust His goodness. Then I suffer the consequences. Proverbs 3:5-6 gently reminds us, *"Trust in the Lord with all your heart, and do not lean on your own understanding. In all your ways acknowledge Him, and He will make your paths straight."*

Does this reflect the confident trust of a beloved child, or the reluctant surrender of a wounded heart? Often, I don't trust God's heart for me. Maybe you can relate. Perhaps your image of God is a cold, hard-hearted bully, or a distant, uninterested presence. How can we trust a God like that? But King David didn't see God that way.

## What Was David's Image Of God?

David was called a man after God's own heart. He ran toward God, not away, because he knew God was safe. He could pray prayers like Psalm 139:1-4, 23-24: *"O Lord, you have searched me and you know me... Before a word is on my tongue you know it completely... Search me, O God, and know my heart... lead me in the way everlasting."* David could pray like this because he knew God's heart was good. He wasn't afraid of being searched, even broken, because he trusted God's love.

Bill Hybels (n.d.) speaks of five dangerous prayers: *search me, break me, stretch me, lead me, use me.* If you've been truly blessed, you know this journey: it's hard, but it makes us usable. Yet something in me resists praying like that. Why?

Because sometimes I still don't believe God likes me. I might believe in Him but not feel liked by Him. Reading about someone isn't the same as knowing them. If I imagine God as impatient, judgmental, or disinterested, why would I want to spend time with Him?

The qualities I'd want in a best friend, acceptance, delight, encouragement, are the same ones I long for in God. If I truly believed He was like that, I'd rush into His presence, not out of duty, but delight. David did. Listen to Psalm 103:8-14: *"The Lord is compassionate and gracious, slow to anger, abounding in love... As a father has compassion on his children, so the Lord has compassion on those who fear him."*

David knew a God who delights in flawed people. He knew God wasn't looking for perfection, He was looking for relationship.

## When Disillusionment Leads Home

Sometimes it takes disillusionment or failure, especially in our closest relationships, to help us face the painful truth: our strategies aren't working. God invites us home to our true selves, seen through His eyes. Ernest Boyer, Jr. (cited in Voskamp, n.d.) said: *"God isn't just a belief you agree with. God becomes a real person you know and meet every day."* In time, your strength becomes His strength, and your love becomes His love. You might even find yourself saying: *"I don't just believe in God - I know Him."*

## Distorted Images

Tozer (2017) warns how crucial it is that our idea of God reflects who He truly is. God's ways are beyond our comprehension (Isaiah 55:8-9), yet He makes Himself known to us.
But when our image of God is distorted, so is our view of reality. For example, I once refused to see my son's anger for what it was because I feared that might mean I had failed him. I distorted reality because I was afraid to face it. I wasn't seeing things as they were, I was seeing them through the filter of my own brokenness.

Distorted images of God affect how we relate to Him. *Table 3. Earthly Father vs Heavenly Father* contains statements of how we see our earthly father in relation to our Heavenly Father and how it hinders us receiving the heart of God. If we see God as a bully or a policeman, we may live in fear, shame, or performance-based striving. We may hide, over-function, or run away altogether. Our self-worth plummets, and we may carry a deep sense of unworthiness. But God wants us to know His true heart, a heart that is slow to anger, abounding in love, and overflowing with compassion.

| **EARTHLY FATHER RELATION TO HEAVENLY FATHER**<br>Hindrances to receiving the heart of God | | |
|---|---|---|
| **Father was...** | **Then I think that...** | **Then I think that...** |
| Dismissive | I am worthless | God is not interested in me |
| Distant | I am insignificant | God couldn't care about me |
| Uncommunicative | I do not matter | God does not want to talk to me |
| Un-affirming | I am not acceptable | God does not think I am |

| | | |
|---|---|---|
| | | useful |
| Non-tactile | I am unclean | God won't come close to me |
| Abusive | I cannot trust people (especially those in power) | I cannot trust God (He has power) |
| Argumenta-tive | Conflict is inevitable | God can't be pleased |
| Violent | People can hurt me | God will hurt me if I am wrong |
| Selfish | I am a second-class citizen | God will 'use me' for His ends |
| Neglectful | My needs do not matter | God will not provide for me |
| Unloving | I am unlovable | God can't love me |
| Harsh | I must deserve punishment | God is a fierce judge with a big stick |
| Critical | I will never be good enough | God sets impossible standards |
| Judgmental | I am inferior to others | I will never be a good Christian |
| Controlling | I am unable to think for myself | God wants to control me |
| Overprotect-ive | I will fail if I try | God always restricts me |
| Spoiling | I can have all I want | God is my 'Sugar Daddy' |
| Unpredict-able | I do not know how to get it right | God will not be consist-ent |

*Table 3.* Earthly Father vs Heavenly Father

## A Gentle Return

It's not easy to heal distorted images of God. But the veil lifts with honesty, with naming the wounds and the false images they birthed. Healing also begins with desire: a longing to know God as He truly is, not as we've imagined Him to be.

Jesus came to reveal the Father's heart, a heart of mercy, tenderness, and fierce love. When Philip asked, *"Show us the Father,"* Jesus replied, *"Anyone who has seen me has seen the Father"* (John 14:9). The more we look at Jesus, the clearer our vision becomes. As we allow His Spirit to speak truth to our hearts, the fog begins to lift. We begin to see, not just intellectually, but experientially, that God is good. That He delights in us. That He is for us.

Sometimes healing happens in a flash. Other times, it comes slowly, through therapy, prayer, trusted relationships, and the faithful presence of God in the ordinary. But it will come. We can trust the One who comes looking for us, not with judgment or shame, but with open arms. We can risk believing that we are not alone. We can learn, at last, to call Him Abba.

## Closing Thoughts

Healing the image of God that we carry within us is a slow, often painful journey. It's one that invites us to look deeper, to confront the distortions shaped by our past, and to allow God to gently reintroduce Himself. The process can feel like peeling back layers, some familiar, some uncomfortable, but each layer, in its own time, reveals a clearer vision of who He truly is.

For so long, I lived with a view of God filtered through the brokenness of my early experiences. I struggled to trust His goodness, His nearness, and His love. It was easier to hold onto the lies, to believe that He was distant, withholding, or maybe even angry with me. But even in those spaces of fear and distance, God was present, quietly inviting me to see Him differently. He never demanded perfection from me, just honesty, just willingness to allow the Holy Spirit to illuminate the truth.

As I reflect on this journey, I realize that healing is not always a moment of sudden clarity, but a gradual unfolding, a series of moments where His love meets me in the midst of my questions, my doubts, and my longing. In each of those moments, I am gently reminded that I am not alone in this process. God is not distant, nor is He disinterested in my pain. His heart is for me, even when I don't feel it. And over time, that truth, though it may start as a whisper, becomes a resounding reality.

If you too have wrestled with an image of God that feels distant or harsh, know that you are not the only one. The longing for a deeper connection with Him is not something to ignore. It is the sign of a heart that was made to know Him truly. Our wounds do not define us; they are places where God is drawing near, offering His healing and His embrace.

This journey of transformation may take time, but it will come. God is faithful, and His desire for relationship with us is constant. Every step forward is a step into the freedom of being fully seen, fully known, and fully loved. In the quiet, in the waiting, in the moments of surrender, we find the deep assurance that we are never truly alone. We are His beloved, and He is our Father.

So, let us come, not as we wish we were, but as we are. With our brokenness, our doubts, and our questions. Let us rest in His love, knowing that He sees us, that He welcomes us, and that He is, always, waiting to restore us, one step, one encounter, one whisper at a time.

And yet, even as we seek His presence, the question arises: *Is God truly who He says He is?* For many, the journey to healing is intertwined with this fundamental question of God's goodness. When we face the depths of our pain, we wrestle with whether His love is truly as deep as He claims, and whether He is as trustworthy as He promises. In the next chapter, we will delve into this question: *The Question of Goodness: Is God Truly Who He Says He Is?* It's a question that speaks to the heart of who we believe God to be and how that belief shapes our journey of healing and restoration.

---

## Declarations

I declare that since I am heirs of God and co-heirs with Christ Jesus, God is good. I am equipped with God's goodness, and I am competent for every good work (2 Timothy 3:17).

I declare that I shall look upon the goodness of the Lord in the land of the living (Psalm 27:13).

I declare that God's goodness and mercy shall follow me all the days of my life: and I will dwell in the house of the LORD forever (Psalms 23:6).

---

## Prayer

*The majesty of God*
*Cannot be measured*
*By human instruments,*
*Cannot be constrained*
*Within human boundaries,*
*Cannot be contained*
*Within human vessels,*
*Cannot be explained*
*By human thought,*
*Cannot be dismissed*
*By argument or reason.*
*The majesty of God*
*Is beyond human comprehension.*
*Yet can be known,*
*And touched,*
*Understood,*
*And received,*

*In the simple act*
*Of worship*
(John Birch, *Faith and Worship*)

---

## Reflection Questions

1. How is your image of God shaped by early relationships with primary caregivers?
2. In what ways do your distorted images of God impact your spiritual wellbeing, self-esteem, and close relationships?
3. You may agree that you are loved by a good God, but do you struggle to feel truly liked by Him? How?
4. What does it mean to surrender wholeheartedly to God, knowing that you are in safe hands?
5. What do you want to talk to God about? (Write or draw a response.)

---

## Journal Prompt

Reflect on a time when you struggled to trust God's heart for you. What did that experience reveal about the distorted images you may have had of Him? Let your pen move without censoring. See what flows out.

# CHAPTER 14

## *Is God Truly Good? My Wrestling with His Character*

---

> *"When you are very still in a place without words, steeped in silence, when the world is elsewhere with its noise and motion, what are the sacred hungers that echo inside of you?" ~ Dawna Markova, I Will Not Die an Unlived Life*
>
> *"Trauma is when pain overwhelms us. Awe is when God overwhelms us. Which is why awe heals trauma: our deep pain is overwhelmed by our great God." ~ Ann Voskamp*
>
> *"Earthly things must be known to be loved; Divine things must be loved to be known." ~ Blaise Pascal*

---

### When Survival Demands Agreement With A Lie

There are wounds so deep, they don't just alter how we see ourselves, they distort how we see God. In the wake of trauma, abandonment, or betrayal, our survival instincts often lead us to conclusions that feel necessary at the time but quietly reshape our theology. If God is good, why didn't He stop it? If He loves me, why did He feel so absent? These aren't just philosophical questions. They are cries from a wounded soul trying to make sense of suffering.

In my own journey, I came to realize I had formed hidden agreements, not only about myself but about God. They were quiet, subconscious, and deeply rooted in pain. *God is distant. God is demanding. God cares more about obedience than my heart.* While I did not vocalize them, they influenced my prayers, trust, and relationship with Him internally.

Wrestling with God's character isn't rebellion. It's relationship. It's the kind of sacred honesty God invites. In this chapter, I open the door to my own struggle, my questions, disillusionment, and the slow, sometimes painful return to a God who is far better than the lies I believed. This is not a tidy testimony of resolution, but a path forged in the tension between sorrow and trust.

## The Cycle Of Shame And Despair

During a particularly painful time in my life, I felt like I had reached the end of myself. I was deeply ashamed of my failure and felt like the ground had disappeared beneath me. All I could see was pain, darkness, and silence from heaven. I didn't want to live anymore. I cried out, but God felt far away. I searched his Word for comfort, but it left me cold. Friends prayed, and I listened to worship music until the words became noise. I remembered verses about God being close to the brokenhearted, but all I could feel was distance.

The spiral of shame was familiar:

> First came the sense of failure.
> Then came the feeling of being exposed.
> Then profound shame (*"This is who I am, a failure"*).
> Then despair (*"Here I am again; nothing will change; there is no hope"*).
> Then came the strong desire to end it all.

This wasn't just disappointment, it was despair. It wasn't just sadness, it was hopelessness. The weight of it crushed me.

## The God I Couldn't Trust

As a child, my mother conveyed a powerful message to me that people would be better off without me. That wound, deep and wordless, distorted how I saw God. At a subconscious level, I believed that God tolerated me but did not delight in me. That he used me, but didn't treasure me. So, when I failed, I expected him to walk away.

In that moment of collapse, I could no longer pretend I trusted his heart. The image of God I had inherited was one of demand, not delight; silence, not presence; judgment, not mercy. My theology told me God was good. My experience told me he had left me.

I asked myself hard questions. Why was I always the one reaching for God? Why did he feel close to others and silent to me? I remembered praying with all my heart and feeling nothing in return. Was God even listening? I wanted to believe, but my faith felt thin, like paper in the rain.

## The Cry Of Job And The Nature Of Surrender

I found unexpected comfort in Job. He didn't pretend. He grieved, he raged, he despaired. He had lived with reverence yet lost everything. His friends gave him neat theological answers, but they only deepened his pain. What moved me was his honesty, *"Though he slay me, yet will I hope in him"* (Job 13:15).

I wasn't there yet. I wasn't hoping. I was pleading. And then accusing. And then falling silent. I didn't want neat answers. I wanted presence. I wanted love. I wanted to be held.
Eventually, I found myself reading Job's declaration, *"Naked I came from my mother's womb, and naked I will depart. The Lord gave and the Lord has taken away; blessed be the name of the Lord."* (Job 1:21)

And I wept. I had prayed, *"The Lord gave and then disappeared."* But Job still trusted. In his rawness and reverence, he blessed. And slowly, painfully, I began to see... His silence wasn't absence. It was invitation.

## Knowing Christ: Our Determined Purpose

The Lord began to invite me to let go of my demands and my need for clarity. He called me instead to surrender. Not because I understood, but because I trusted his goodness.
I began to see that God wasn't asking me to have answers. He was asking me to let him hold my questions.

As I read Paul's letter to the Philippians, his words burned through me:

> *"I consider everything a loss compared to the surpassing greatness of knowing Christ Jesus my Lord, for whose sake I have lost all things. I consider them rubbish, that I may gain Christ and be found in him..." (Philippians 3:8–9)*

In *The Message*, Paul says:

> *"Compared to the high privilege of knowing Christ Jesus as my Master firsthand, everything I once thought I had going for me is insignificant, dog dung. I've dumped it all in the trash so that I could embrace Christ and be embraced by him."*

Paul had a determined purpose: to know Christ, even in suffering. Not to use Christ. Not to perform for Christ. Not even to be blessed by Christ, but to know him. *What "dog dung" am I still clinging to as if it will give me life?*

## The Poor In Spirit And The Way Of The Cross

Jesus said, *"Blessed are the poor in spirit, for theirs is the kingdom of heaven"* (Matthew 5:3). The same word for *"poor"* could be translated *"beggar"*, literally, *"to make oneself little; to crouch; a broken and contrite heart."* Jesus proclaims that to be poor in spirit is the primary characteristic of a spiritual heart. Can you imagine Jesus' disciples' reaction when they heard this? Happy and poor do not tend to mix.

The Message translation captures this as, *"You're blessed when you're at the end of your rope. With less of you there is more of God and his rule."* Poverty of spirit is not weakness. It's the surrender of self-sufficiency. It's the end of pretending. It's the honest cry: *"I have nothing to offer. I need you."*

The kingdom doesn't come to the self-righteous. It comes to the broken, the weary, the crushed. The ones who know they cannot save themselves. The ones who have stopped striving.

I had to lay down my shame-driven striving to prove my worth. I had to surrender the lie that I was only valuable if I got it right. I had to stop trying to be good enough and let God be good.

## The Altar Of Surrender

The turning point came not when I felt better, but when I surrendered. I knelt in the silence and said, *"Even if I never feel you again, I will stay. I am yours."* It wasn't a victorious moment. It was a dying one. I laid my distorted image of God on the altar. I laid my wounded heart there too. And in that surrender, I began to taste freedom. I began to know, not just believe, but know that God was not far off. He was with me. Not because I was worthy. But because he is Love.

## What Is Surrender?

What comes to mind with word surrender? Try doing a mind map like the one I did, only with your words (see Figure 4. *Mind*

*Map*).

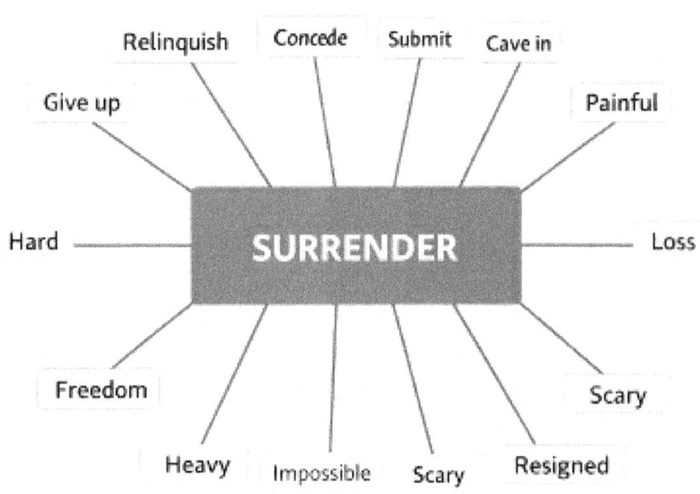


Figure 4. *Mind Map*

According to the Merriam-Webster Dictionary (n.d.), it means *"to yield to the possession or power of another; to give (oneself) up, especially to give up, abandon, or relinquish; to yield; submit."* Honestly, I don't like the sound of that. I prefer not to give someone that much control over me. My past experiences have taught me that surrender can feel like erasure, that if I give myself completely to another, I might lose myself altogether.

Perhaps my greatest obstacle to surrender isn't willpower, but my image of God, especially the image that surfaces in the wake of disappointment, pain, and broken dreams. In those moments, I find myself asking, maybe you do too: *"Is God really good? Does He truly have my best interests at heart? Is He actually trustworthy?"*

Trust, as the dictionary defines it, is the ability to *"hope and rely on someone's character and attributes."* But when our internal world has been shaped by unreliable caregivers, unmet needs, or painful betrayals, this kind of trust doesn't come naturally. So much time and energy can be spent fighting God, plotting our own course, seeking to find significance and security in our achievements or our relationships, and growing resentful when our efforts don't bring the satisfaction we long for. These are the hallmarks of a life not yet surrendered. A self-made world can feel safer because we control it. But it's also exhausting, and in the end, it leaves us hollow.

Still, *God pursues us.*

For a long time, I thought surrender meant kneeling at the altar with my burdens, laying down my worries, offering my worship. I thought that was enough. But now I realise God doesn't just want my burdens on the altar, as Nelson (2002, p. 94) writes, *"God wants* me *to be on the altar with them."*

Jesus is our model of what that looks like. He was entirely surrendered to His Father, not just in action but in posture, in heart. The heart of Christianity is found in God's selfless, humble nature, revealed in Jesus Christ. This humility is not weakness but the courageous vulnerability of love. God is kenotic, self-emptying, always giving, compassionate, and intimately involved in the world. God's vulnerability does not waver. He enters our suffering, remains with us in the ache of loss, and births new life from places of barrenness and abandonment. His commitment is not only to confront our pain, but to carry it with us, and through it, to bring hope, joy, and resurrection life.

Jesus willingly gave up the right to use His power, to be esteemed, to win. He didn't assert dominance; He laid down His rights. As Nelson (2002, pp. 89, 92) reflects, Jesus surrendered even His right to be respected. He refused to use His power in ways that would harm, control, or manipulate. Instead, He surrendered His will entirely to the Father.

## Job's Plight

There's a well-known story in the Old Testament about a righteous man named Job who lost everything, his wealth, his health, his children. But the greatest agony of Job, and of anyone who has suffered deep loss, wasn't the pain itself. It was the apparent meaninglessness of it all.

We don't know what to do with unjust suffering. We don't know what to do with a silent God. Where is God when we hurt? Why does He allow suffering? These may be the most primal questions we ever ask. At the heart of human existence is this: *Who is God, and who are we before Him?* And where is He when life collapses?

When my own life has fallen apart, I've felt overwhelmed and claustrophobic, like I was imploding in on myself. Pain becomes the whole world, and the temptation is to believe that this private hell is all there ever was, is, and will be.

But Job (1:21–22, MSG) responded to his devastation in a way that's almost implausible:

> *"Naked I came from my mother's womb,*
> *and naked I'll return to the womb of the earth.*
> *God gives, God takes.*
> *God's name be ever blessed."*

Not once through all this did Job sin; not once did he blame God.
Even in the wreckage, Job's image of God remained: a God who is good and trustworthy. Job knew who he was before that God, naked, vulnerable, weak, broken.

Unbeknown to him, a wager had taken place in heaven:

> *"Do you think Job does all that out of the sheer goodness*

> *of his heart?" Satan sneered. "You pamper him like a pet! Bless everything he touches, of course he trusts you. But take it all away, and he'll curse you to your face" (Job 1:9–10, MSG).*

Job refused to curse God, even when his wife gave in. Job didn't deny his suffering, but he didn't let it distort his view of God.

## Covering Our Nakedness

Job accepted his nakedness before God. But what about us? What emotional fig leaves do we use to cover our vulnerability? What do we use to define ourselves, relationships, children, achievements, wealth, intelligence, insight, status, friends? I've hidden behind all of these at times. And like Job's friends, I've sometimes responded to suffering by grasping for certainty.

## The Sin Of Job's Friends

At one time, I believed I was like Job. But I've come to realize that I've also been like his friends. They weren't wrong in what they said; many of their words were theologically sound. Their sin was in what they *assumed*: that suffering must always be the result of sin, that God always operates in predictable ways.

Their need to defend their image of God caused them to speak falsely on His behalf. They made God manageable, boxed Him up into a tidy theological system that protected them from the discomfort of mystery.

I've done this too, clinging to knowledge as a way to keep pain at bay, turning faith into certainty, rather than trust. When we shrink God to fit inside our constructs, He stops being God. Our image of Him becomes our idol. Then when tragedy strikes, we interpret it through that false image, and our faith crumbles. That's what happened to me.

## Job's Encounter With God

Job journeyed through unrelenting pain, clinging to his innocence, pleading for a hearing with God. His friends hammered him for twenty-three chapters, and still he held his ground:

> *"Let the Almighty answer me," he cried. "Let me see the charges against me!" Then, finally, God speaks. "Who is this that obscures my plans with words without knowledge? Brace yourself like a man; I will question you, and you shall answer me" (Job 38:1).*

This is no gentle whisper. God speaks from a whirlwind. His words are not comforting. He doesn't explain Himself. He doesn't answer Job's questions. He doesn't mention the wager with Satan.

Instead, He asks His own questions, dozens of them. Sarcastic, sweeping, fierce questions. Job is undone.

> *"I'm speechless, in awe, words fail me.*
> *I should never have opened my mouth!*
> *I've talked too much, way too much.*
> *I'm ready to shut up and listen" (Job 40:4–5, MSG).*

God continues, and when He finishes, Job is transformed.

> *"I'm convinced: You can do anything and everything. Nothing and no one can upset Your plans. I babbled on about things far beyond me... I admit I once lived by rumors of You; now I have it firsthand, from my own eyes and ears. I'm sorry, forgive me. I'll never again live on crumbs of hearsay" (Job 42:1–6, adapted MSG).*

Job never receives an explanation. He doesn't get answers, he gets God. And somehow, that is enough.

## Letting God Be God

What's astonishing is that while Job was on trial, so was God. The core question beneath his suffering wasn't, *"Why me?"* but: *Is God worthy of worship, even when everything is lost? Is God still good when I have nothing left to thank Him for?* Job's eventual answer is yes. And through the stripping, the silence, the storm, he meets God, not as an idea, but as a Presence.

I have known this place too, where suffering strips you of your fig leaves, your formulas, your spiritual performance. Where God doesn't answer your questions but makes Himself known.

## The Mystery Of Suffering

God never told Job about Satan's wager. He never explained the reason for his suffering. Some things belong to the mystery of God and will only be revealed at the end of the age.
Hebrews 11 describes those who lived by faith yet never received what was promised. *"They saw it and welcomed it from a distance."* I, too, want to know now. I want to skip the waiting, the unknowing.

But transformation doesn't come that way. As Milne put it:

> *"How does one become a butterfly?" Pooh asked pensively.*
> *"You must want to fly so much that you are willing to give up being a caterpillar," Piglet replied.*
> *"You mean to die?" asked Pooh.*
> *"Yes and no," said Piglet. "What looks like you will die, but what's really you will live on."*

## The Mystery Of God: Trusting In His Goodness Amid Suffering

In Isaiah 46:10, God declares, *"I make known the end from the beginning, from ancient times, what is still to come. I say: My purpose will stand, and I will do all that I please."* This verse is a reminder of the vastness of God's plans, far beyond our comprehension. The Scriptures frequently speak of God's depth and mystery, His ways are higher, His judgments beyond our understanding:

- *"The Spirit knows everything, even the deepest secrets of God."* (1 Corinthians 2:10)
- *"Oh, how rich and wise is God's understanding! His judgments are beyond our grasp, and His ways are impossible to trace."* (Romans 11:33)
- *"Can you comprehend the mysteries of God? Can you understand the limits of the Almighty? They are higher than the heavens, what can you do? They are deeper than the depths of the earth, what can you know?"* (Job 11:7-8)

So, if God is so deep, so unfathomable, why should we even try to know Him, or love Him with our whole being? If we can't grasp His essence, how can we trust Him with our lives?

## A Relationship Beyond The Obvious

The invitation to know God is not about intellectual mastery. It is about relationship. Though He operates in realms beyond our understanding, God longs for us to explore and experience the treasures hidden in the depths. *"You cannot know God until you've stopped telling yourself that you already know God"* (Walsch, 1995). This is not an intellectual pursuit, but a relational one, one that requires us to surrender the illusion of control and discover God in ways we never expected.

## The Character Of God: Is He Trustworthy?

Is God good? Is He trustworthy? Can I trust Him with my life and everything I hold dear? These questions sound simple, but they are far from easy. God has declared His goodness, He loves us, He knows what is best for us, and He has the power to accomplish it. But trusting in His goodness means surrendering our own independent, often sinful, ways of controlling life.

The true test of trust is not just in believing in God's goodness, but in answering the difficult question: *"Is there anything I could lose that would make me stop trusting God?"* This is a severe question. In the book of Job, we see a man who endured suffering that seemed unreasonable, cruel, and beyond what anyone should have to bear. Yet Job's journey shows us that it is only through suffering that we learn to relinquish control. As Richard Rohr (2009) writes, suffering can be defined as *"when you're not in control."* It is through suffering that we learn to let go and trust in something far greater than ourselves.

## The Transformative Power Of Suffering

Pain and suffering can be transformative if we allow God to work through them. Job's story illustrates this, his suffering did not have easy answers, but it was the very thing that broke open his image of God. Had he pulled back too soon, the story of Job would never have unfolded as it did. Through his struggle, Job came to know a deeper, truer God, one who was both mysterious and trustworthy.

I too have wrestled with similar thoughts, wondering if God was playing with me, dangling me over the abyss. There have been times when I've believed God was a sadist, tormenting me by threatening to take away the things I love most. But as I look back now, I realize that had I pulled back in those moments, I would never have tasted the sweetness of knowing God in a new and more profound way.

### The Final Analysis: God's Pursuit of Us

In the final analysis, God comes to us disguised as our lives. Rohr puts it this way: *"God comes to us disguised as our life."* He enters our deepest struggles, our worst pain, and our most helpless moments, not to punish us, but to transform us. Job's story ends with him dying old and full of days, but the journey to that end was marked by a complete shift in his understanding of God. Job never knew why he suffered, but he found peace in the mystery. He learned that God was bigger, wilder, and more trustworthy than he ever imagined. Job no longer needed to understand why; he had come to trust that God is ultimately in control.

Romans 8:28 reassures us of this truth: *"We can be so sure that every detail in our lives of love for God is worked into something good."* Even when we cannot see the path forward, we can trust that God is at work. The Psalmist reminds us: *"Surely Your goodness and unfailing love will pursue me all the days of my life..."* (Psalm 23:6). The Hebrew word for "follow" here, *radaph*, means *"to pursue, to run after, to chase"*, to hunt down (Strong, 1990). It is a relentless, passionate pursuit of our hearts. God is not standing back, waiting for us to fail. He is chasing us down with love and grace, seeking to bless us, even when we feel undeserving.

## Learning From The Butterflies

I recall a visit to a Butterfly Farm in Thailand with my daughter. We watched in awe as the butterflies danced from one flower to the next, free and light, trusting that their needs would be met. They didn't try to control their lives, they simply lived in the moment, allowing God to guide their flight. There is so much we can learn from the butterflies. True freedom, true trust, is found not in control, but in surrender. When we let go of the need to understand everything and trust God with our lives, we experience the freedom of His peace.

## Closing Thoughts

In the end, the journey of knowing God is not about unravelling all the mysteries of His being. It's about learning to trust in the goodness and wisdom of a God whose ways are beyond our understanding. We may never have all the answers, and we may not always comprehend why suffering enters our lives. But we can trust in the One who holds all things in His hands, who pursues us with unfailing love, and who promises to work all things for good.

As we journey through life, God invites us to step into the mystery, not with fear, but with awe and wonder. Like Job, we may face moments where our faith is tested to its limits, but if we allow God to meet us in those spaces, we will emerge transformed. Our image of Him will grow deeper and richer. Our trust will be strengthened. And we will find that, even in the unknown, God is more trustworthy than we ever imagined.

So, let us embrace the unknowns, the mysteries, and the unanswered questions, knowing that in every moment of life, whether in joy or suffering, God is pursuing us with a love that never fails. May we learn, like the butterfly, to live in freedom, trusting that the One who holds the universe also holds our hearts.

But for many of us, the journey toward trusting God is complicated by the layers of shame we carry, shame that distorts our perception of both ourselves, and Him. Shame doesn't just shape how we see ourselves; it shapes how we see God. The unloved self often projects its fears and unmet needs onto the divine, creating an image of God that echoes the pain we've experienced in our early relationships. These projections, whether God is distant, harsh, or impossible to please, form the walls of protection we build around our hearts. Before we can truly trust God's heart, we must uncover how our image of Him has been warped by the wounds of shame. In the next chapter, we will explore this complex and painful process in greater depth: *Shame's Many Faces: Understanding the Layers of Wounding.*

---

## Declarations

I declare that God is the one true God. He is good, showing forth His love, His truth, His goodness, righteousness, and sovereignty both to me and to the World!

I declare that His love and compassion reside within me.

I declare that his divine power has given me everything I need for a godly life through our knowledge of him who called me by his own glory and goodness.

I declare that God's face is smiling toward me, and He longs to be good to me.

---

## Prayer

*I ask You, God, the glorious Father of our Lord Jesus Christ, to give me spiritual wisdom and insight so that I might grow in the knowledge of God (Ephesians 3:17). I want to learn to trust you, so I am asking You today to open up my heart that I might know you in all your mystery and wonder. I believe that You are loving and kind and desire for me to be Your friend. I am hungry for You. I ask you to be Lord of my life, to teach me heal me and free me. Through Your strength, may I become the person you designed me to be. I desire to be used in this world to bless and heal others. So, I ask for and expect transformation, peace and joy from your hand as I walk with You each day and seek to serve You with a whole heart.*

---

## Reflection Questions

1. What distorted image of God am I holding onto when life falls apart?

2. Where am I resisting surrender out of fear that God is not good?

3. Do you lean more towards Job or his friends? Can you explain why?

4. How do you understand the idea of suffering?

5. Have you ever experienced pain or suffering, and how did God help you through it?

---

## Journal Prompt

Reflect on a time when you wrestled with trusting God. What did you learn about His character and your own in that process? Let your pen move without censoring. See what flows out.

# CHAPTER 15

## The Faces of Shame

---

*"It you attempt to act and do for others or for the world without deepening your own self-understanding, freedom, integrity and capacity to love, you will not have anything to give others. You will communicate to them nothing but the contagion of your own obsessions, your aggressivity, your ambitions, your delusions and ends and means..." ~ Thomas Merton*

*"Many Christians... find themselves defeated by the most psychological weapon that Satan uses against them. This weapon has the effectiveness of a deadly missile. Its name? Low self-esteem. Satan's greatest psychological weapon is a gut level feeling of inferiority, inadequacy, and low self-worth This feeling shackles many Christians, in spite of wonderful spiritual experiences and knowledge of God's Word. Although they understand their position as sons and daughters of God, they are tied up in knots, bound by a terrible feeling inferiority, and chained to a deep sense of worthlessness." ~ David Seamands, Healing for Damaged Emotions*

*"I sought the Lord, and he answered me and delivered me from all my fears. Those who look to him are radiant, and their faces shall never be ashamed." ~ Psalm 34:4-5*

---

## Shame's Power

The gentle, insightful man praying for me places his hand on my head. As he prays, I see in my mind's eye two little girls. One is three, the other seven. They are hiding in a dark place, tucked away where no one can see them. It feels safer that way. Outside their hiding place stands Jesus, arms open, eyes kind, a gentle smile playing on His lips. He beckons the children to come. But they are too afraid. Still, Jesus waits. He does not leave. He is infinitely patient.

Eventually, the older girl peeks out. "Is it safe?" she whispers. Jesus smiles and nods. She steps out, and with her, the younger one follows. They run into His arms, and He sweeps them up, holding them close. He speaks soothing words, pouring His love into their hungry, aching hearts.

Those little girls are me.

## Shame: The Silent Companion

Growing up, shame became my closest companion. I wore it like a heavy cloak, a second skin. My parents' generation often used shame as a motivator. I suspect they too were shaped by it, wounded by their own parents and passing it on, unaware. Shame is a legacy unless someone breaks the cycle.

Fossum and Mason (1989) describe it as a cloak that renders a person worthless and isolated. It happens when a parent violates or diminishes the child's personhood, sometimes blatantly, sometimes subtly. Perhaps they overvalue independence, denying the child's need for connection. Or perhaps they smother with overdependence, denying the child's need for separateness. Either way, an essential part of the child is ignored, dismissed, or shamed.

To be shamed is to be executed for a crime you did not commit, only it is the self that dies.

## The Weapon Of Shaming

Shame was the sharpest weapon in my mother's arsenal. When her fury descended, I feared annihilation. Her message was clear: I was nothing, a nobody. And if my own mother couldn't love me, then surely, I was unlovable. Something must be terribly wrong with me.
I buried that shameful belief deep, but I buried it alive.

Brené Brown (2012), in her TED Talk *Listening to Shame*, says shame needs three things to survive: secrecy, silence, and judgment. I had all three. My secrets infected every relationship, especially my relationship with myself. Perhaps because they masked unbearable emotions: sadness, loneliness, heartache, abandonment, resentment, fear. To survive, I shut down. I hid. I forfeited authenticity to stay safe.

## Conversion Didn't Erase Shame

At twenty-one, I entrusted my life to Jesus. I wish I could say shame vanished then, but it didn't. My conversion was real, but the spirituality I was taught to live out was externally defined. In earlier chapter, I spoke of how this worked. Follow the rules. Choose the right behaviour. Put the coin in, get the blessing out. God was portrayed more like a cosmic vending machine than a loving Father. In this system, appearances mattered more than inner truth. So, I covered myself with the proverbial fig leaf. Behind the leaf, a broken heart wept.

There was little room for self-reflection. I feared facing my story because I thought it would confirm the lie that I already believed that my presence caused pain, that everything was my fault. My mother's voice echoed still. And so, I remained disconnected from my own story. Yet the Gospel is about heart restoration. But shame had burrowed deep into my core, stealing life itself.

## The Breaking

The turning point came at twenty-eight. My heart broke, utterly, devastatingly. It had been coming for a while - weight loss, bone-deep exhaustion, an ache I couldn't name. I felt bludgeoned by life, helpless, out of control. And then came the final blow, words from my husband's family: *"Look what you're doing to us. Shame on you. Pull yourself together."* I absorbed their judgment, internalised it, and slid further into despair.

Church folks were no different. Rules kept them safe from themselves and from people like me. Their eyes said it all: discomfort, pity, withdrawal. Their spiritual masks kept my pain at a distance. One pastor visited me in hospital. He couldn't even meet my gaze. *"What can I tell you that you don't already know?"* he mumbled and disappeared from my life.

Despair became a prison. Connection felt impossible. The ache of loss, loneliness, and disappointment was excruciating. So, I shut down. I deadened desire and hope. The enemy whispered: *"Expect nothing and you won't be disappointed."* I believed the lie. Depression became my only escape. Not from life, but from the agony of existing.

Dan Allender (2015) calls despair a flight from desire. It's a refusal to accept loss and the emptiness that could make room for God. Despair cannot dream. It runs to the false safety of numbness. A place where the fantasy of not existing is preferable to risking more pain. In that place, I held a photo of my children and decided they'd be better off without me. I tried to disappear.

## A Hand In Mine

Years later, I'm in a Tuk-Tuk in Sri Lanka, bumping along dusty roads after ministering to war-traumatised Tamils. Next to me sits a young man, maybe nineteen. He's a teammate on the ministry trip. He slips his hand into mine, looks into my eyes, and says, *"Will you be my mother? I love you."*

Tears spring to my eyes. *"I love you too,"* I whisper. *"I would be honoured to be your mother."*

He lost his birth mother during the brutal civil war. Instead of comfort, his family shamed him: *"Look at you, motherless boy. It's your fault she died. Who will want you now?"* Shame split his heart wide open. It told him he was disgusting, worthless, unlovable. He bore a wound that was not his fault, but he paid the price anyway. Shame shaped his entire being. It made him hide, not heal. It told him who he was, not who God said he was. How do we recover from shame that deep? How do we reclaim the truth of who we are?

## Understanding Shame

Shame has been called the most corrosive of human emotions. Judith Herman (2006) describes it as an intense, overwhelming experience that triggers the body's fight-or-flight response. Budden (2009) adds that shame can range from mild embarrassment to severe humiliation, and it always involves the fear of being exposed as *"not enough."* The Merriam-Webster dictionary defines shame as *"dishonour or disgrace."* But shame is more than a word, it is a wound on the soul.

Kaufman (2004) suggests that shame is like a shy little creature, hiding in the shadows, afraid to be seen. There's no adequate scientific language to describe its inner experience. But its presence is unmistakable.

Henri Nouwen (2002) observed that the greatest trap in life is not success, fame, or power, but self-rejection. And when that rejection comes from within, it is devastating. *"What if the critical voice in your head is right?"* asks Cloud and Townsend (2017). *"What if you are the problem?"* That is the voice of the enemy, the accuser who delights in shame, who seeks to divide and isolate us from God and one another.

## The Roots Of Shame

Shame can come from without or within. Gilbert (2003) notes that externally, shame is passed on as perceived rejection. Internally, it is self-judgment, often moral, often harsh.
It is socially constructed, says Schore (1994), and passed down in families and cultures. A child doesn't need to be told they're shameful. They absorb it through tone, posture, gaze.
Budden (2009) describes the *"safety behaviours"* of shame: slumped posture, avoiding eye contact, turning away, zoning out. Outward submission. Inward hiding.

Understanding how shame develops is the first step toward freedom. Only then can we begin to see ourselves as God sees us. And that changes everything.

## Closing Thoughts

So, let us choose to shed the cloak of shame and wear the mantle of God's love. Let us walk in the freedom He offers, knowing that we are fully known and fully loved, just as we are. This is the heart of healing, the freedom to be, to love, to embrace both our brokenness and our beauty in the light of God's grace.

But this journey doesn't begin with self-acceptance alone, it begins with truth. Before we can embrace the love of God, we must first recognize the ways shame has shaped our inner world. The child who hides in shame becomes the adult who fears that God is angry, distant, or impossible to please. If our early caregivers distorted the image of love, that distortion becomes the lens through which we see God, and ourselves. These false images bury the truth of our belovedness, and feed our silent fears of rejection, inadequacy, and isolation.

Shame doesn't just touch the surface of our identity; it seeps deep into the soul, warping our sense of worth and twisting our view of love. It whispers that we are unworthy, unlovable, beyond repair. And unless we name those lies and bring them into the light, they will continue to echo through our relationships, our faith, and our self-perception.

In the next chapter, we take a deeper look at this internal struggle. *The Unloved Self: How Shame Warps the Soul* invites us to uncover how these deep wounds form, how they affect our relationship with God and others, and how healing can begin, not by striving for perfection, but by allowing ourselves to be seen, known, and loved in the places we've most wanted to hide.

---

## Declarations

I declare that I am beloved by God, not because of my performance, but because of His unchanging love. I am worthy of His love and grace, and I choose to step out of hiding and into the freedom of being fully known and fully loved.

I declare that shame no longer has a hold on my heart. I reject the lies that tell me I am unworthy, unlovable, or too broken. I choose to see myself through God's eyes, as His child, precious and redeemed by the blood of Christ.

I declare that healing is possible, and it begins with embracing God's truth about who I am. I will no longer allow the shadows of shame to isolate me from His love, but I will walk in the light of His grace, free to be my true self, fully accepted and deeply cherished.

---

## Prayer

*Father God, Thank You for Your endless love and grace. I come before You, acknowledging the shame that has burdened my heart for so long. I ask You to heal the wounds of my soul, replacing every lie with the truth of who I am in You. Help me to see myself through Your eyes, loved, valued, and worthy. I surrender my shame to You and invite Your peace to fill the spaces where fear and self-rejection once lived. Thank You for Your patience and for always being with me. In Jesus' name, Amen.*

---

## Reflection Questions

1. How has shame manifested in my life: What specific moments or experiences in my past have shaped my view of myself as unworthy or unlovable?
2. What false beliefs about myself have I internalized because of shame?
3. How do these beliefs affect my relationships with others, with God, and with myself?
4. In what areas of my life do I still find myself hiding or retreating, like the child in the dark place?
5. What would it look like to step out into the light of God's love and truth?
6. How do I view my worth in light of the Gospel: Do I see myself as beloved by God, or do I still struggle with feelings of inferiority or inadequacy?
7. In what ways has shame influenced my ability to give and receive love?
8. How can I begin to accept God's love for me, even when I feel unworthy or broken?

## Journal Prompt

Reflect on a moment when you felt unworthy or shameful. How might God's love and truth rewrite that story for you today? Let your pen move without censoring. See what flows out.

# CHAPTER 16

## *The Self I Rejected*

---

*"To embrace and love who we are, we have to reclaim and reconnect with the parts of ourselves we've orphaned over the years." ~ Brené Brown, Rising Strong*

*"No one who hopes in you will ever be put to shame..." ~ Psalm 25:3*

---

### When Shame Becomes The Story We Live By

There's a kind of pain that doesn't bleed or bruise but buries itself deep within the soul, a quiet ache that whispers: *Something is wrong with me.* It often begins before we have words to name it. A frown, a harsh word, a parent's distraction, or unmet need lodges in the heart and takes root as shame, not the kind that says *I've done something bad,* but the more insidious kind that insists *I am bad.*

Over time, this message becomes a lens, warping how we see ourselves, others, and even God. We learn to hide, to perform, to please, to protect ourselves from ever feeling that unloved self again. But the cost is high. The soul, created for intimacy and delight, is slowly smothered by masks, striving, and isolation. This chapter is about that journey, how shame is born, how it shapes us, and how, by grace, it can be unlearned.

## The Unloved Self In My Story

I didn't have language for shame as a child. I only knew that something in me hurt, something quiet and confusing, like a slow fade of light I hadn't realized I needed to survive.
When I was little, my father was affectionate. I remember his arms around me, his warmth, the sense of being safe in his presence. But as I grew older, that affection slipped away, without explanation. He didn't criticize or correct me; he simply withdrew. And in that silence, I felt the sting of something unnamed.

Was it something I did? Something I became? I internalized the withdrawal not as a change in him, but as a flaw in me. The lack of warmth became a mirror that reflected back the message: *You're no longer enough.* I missed the tenderness I'd once known, and feared it was gone because I had somehow failed to deserve it.

Shame settled quietly in my soul, not as a loud accusation, but as a deep uncertainty about my worth. It coloured the way I approached others, and the way I related to God. I loved Him, yes, but I also feared He might be like my father: present when I was small and innocent, but withdrawing when I grew older, more complicated, more *"me."*

It's taken years, of counselling, prayer, and learning to sit still with my pain, to realize that God doesn't withhold love like that. He doesn't withdraw when I grow or falter or question. He leans in. Even now, He is healing the unloved self in me, not by demanding I try harder, but by inviting me to trust that I am already deeply, fiercely loved.

## How Does Shame Develop?

Understanding the development of shame and how it impacts our identity may help us to see how it restricts an authentic view of ourselves as God sees us. If we lack being seen by One who loves and accepts us as we are, we will continually embark on pain management - destructive, self-protective strategies designed to help us to endure and survive rather than thrive.

The family is the crucible of how to love, be loved, and deal with feelings and beliefs about the self and the world. Sadly, shame often enters through our earliest interactions. As an infant, Laura became attached to the caregiver with whom she had the most interaction, her mother, and she became increasingly effective in seeking and maintaining proximity to her preferred attachment figure (Clinton & Sibcy, 2002).

Stern (2000, p. 72) describes how Laura, beginning at two months and lasting for several months, would be overwhelmingly focused on her mother. In fact, the key to Laura's psychological development is maintaining a strong bond with her parental figure throughout the day and it is perhaps the most exclusively social period of life. Laura's *"first order of business"* is to form *"the sense of a core self and core others"* (Stern, 2000, p. 70). Laura's ability to regulate her emotions is established during this critical time by interactions with her mother and is at the core of the origin of her sense of self.

## The Need For Interactive Repair

When Laura begins to crawl, one of the most important functions of developing healthy emotions is for the primary caregiver (usually the mother) to supervise and intervene in her forays into her surroundings, responding to potentially dangerous situations. When danger halts Laura's explorations and interferes with her previously responsive attachment system, Laura's mother must place limits on her behaviour.

When her mother becomes directive, Laura experiences shame and rejection for the first time, causing a break in the emotional bond. Her mother must now initiate "interactive repair," which involves restoring the emotional connection between her and Laura (Hughes, 2010, p. 18). If the repair is successful, Laura learns to regulate both pleasure and frustration, affection and anger, within herself and in her relationship with her mother.

However, if Laura's mother is not skilled at *"interactive repair"* and shames her infant, Laura will struggle to develop empathy. Her empathic relationship with her mother assists in the development of *"experience-dependent neural pathways,"* particularly in the frontal lobes of the brain (p. 22). If empathy is not modelled during this crucial developmental period, it will be compromised in later life. The principle of *"use it or lose it"* applies.

Moreover, shame is antithetical to empathy and prevents Laura from being empathic toward herself. Shame is a tough feeling. It's like a deep, painful sense of being flawed and unworthy of love and acceptance. It can make you feel scared, blame yourself, and feel disconnected from others (Brown, 2008, p. 29). Consequently, shame-inducing experiences are connected to adult difficulties in interpersonal relationships, empathy, healthy thoughts, impulse control, and aggression regulation.

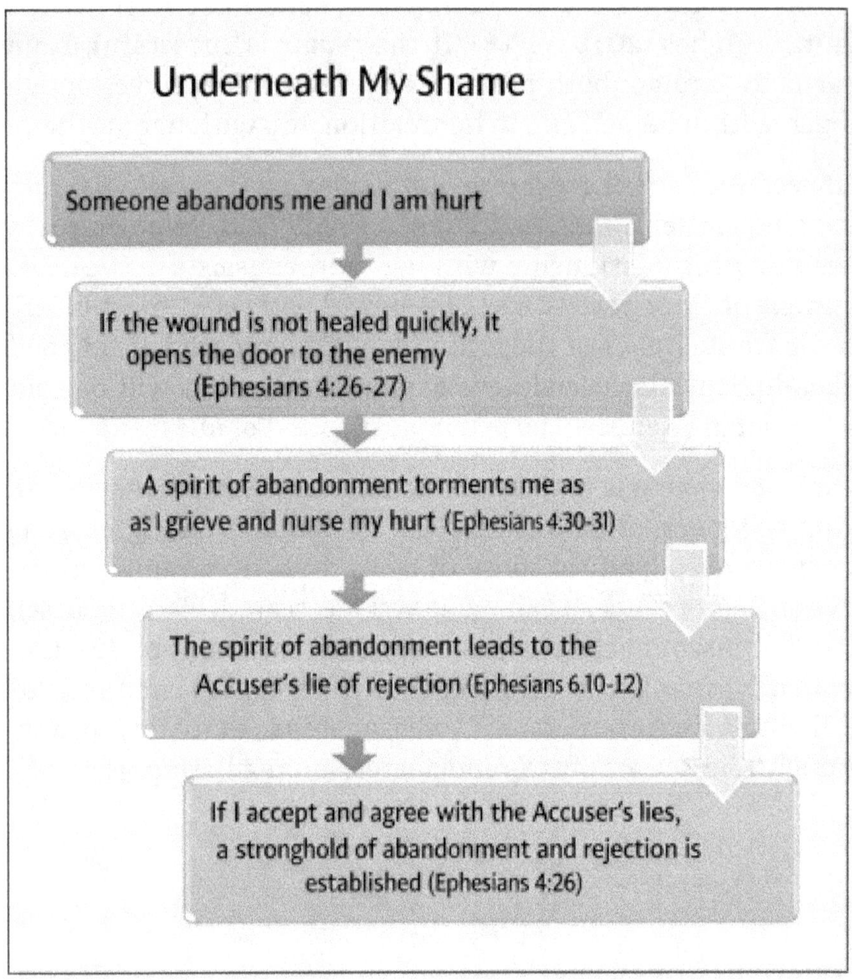


Figure 5. *What Lies Beneath Shame*

Shame leads to the development of experience-dependent neural pathways of self or other contempt. Laura will either attack the self, attack others, or use a combination of both (see Figure 5. *What Lies Beneath Shame*).

## Men, Women And Shame Responses

Shame triggers tend to be different for men and women. Women are bombarded with a complex set of expectations, but there's one thing that seems to be the most important for men, don't show weakness (Brown, 2004). Women tend to feel shame when they perceive they fall short of the standards they impose on themselves. They seek core validation. If it is not forthcoming, they tend to blame themselves and move away from their vulnerability. For example, they long to be a good wife, mother, daughter, sibling, friend, and so on. When these relationships fail, a woman feels she is without a voice, abandoned and unseen. Her response tends to become controlling, demanding, desolate, or needy.

On the other hand, men long to feel that they are courageous, that their words, decisions, and their lives matter and have impact. They tend to feel shame when they sense they have failed or lack the strength to give on behalf of others. For example, a man may respond to an early message of *You are not good enough* by blaming others, using aggression and violence, shutting down, or moving into passivity. Gilligan (2016) says she's never seen a violent act that wasn't triggered by feeling ashamed, humiliated, disrespected, and ridiculed. It's always about trying to save face or undo that *loss of face.* Thus, we often oscillate between being a victim or an offender.

## What Are The Consequences Of Shame?

Shame has far-reaching consequences. When we're hurt or embarrassed, we naturally want to hide our feelings, from God, others, and even ourselves. But here's the catch: hiding our wounds prevents us from healing and growing. What was once a shield for a child can become a prison for an adult (Townsend, 2001).

As an adult, shame and its close cousin, self or other condemnation, will affect Laura in two ways. First, shame originates from what others do to her during her crucial developmental years, and second, condemnation stems from regret over something she does or does not do. Both keep her self-focused and unable to heal.

Shame and condemnation are a kind of death. For example, at a dinner party, I was shamed by a family member in front of others for being fat, even giving me a degrading nickname that stuck. Even though it was not true, strong emotions flooded me abruptly and acutely, as they often do. It was like the ground opened up beneath me and I disappeared into a hole. I was not only humiliated but felt expelled from the human race. In that moment, I knew I would never belong. My deficiency and inadequacy had been publicly exposed, and I was justifiably cast out, alone, cut off, and condemned. There was nothing I could do to set it right.

## A Horrid Email

Another incident was an email that undid me. At the time, several of the men in my life were steeped in avoidance that impeded closeness and authenticity. My pastor and long-time friend refused to admit the truth and denied hurting me, pretending nothing was wrong.

Additionally, the head of the department where I worked refused to take an honest, hard look at how his relational style was alienating his coworkers. Then there was my husband, whose work so absorbed his energy that he had little left for me.

All the important men in my life were disregarding my ache for authentic relationship. When my cries went unheeded, my well ran dry, and I grieved. It was the perfect storm. When the CEO of my Christian workplace denied financial support for my African mission trip (when previously it had been freely given), I sent a contemptuous email accusing him of lacking a kingdom heart. When I pressed send, I did not care about the impact, I wanted to hurt him.

But no sooner had I sent the email than I was inundated with self-condemnation and regret. In that moment, I had forgotten who I was. I lost sight of the other—and the truth that I really did care. I began to feel terrible about myself and tried to hide from the weight of it. What struck me most was the sudden, inescapable awareness of something dark within me, the shame of it. It wasn't just that I had done something bad; I *was* bad. That's how it felt. This sense of badness was confirmed, in my mind, by the look of disgust I saw on his face when our paths later crossed.

Then came his comment: *"I didn't expect that from a counsellor."* Those words cut deep. The message was clear; I was supposed to be above human frailty. I should have known better, done better, because of all I had learned about people. His comment didn't just shame me; it shook me to my core and embedded itself in my heart. For years afterward, I carried it. I still cringe when I recall the incident.

Even though I offered a heartfelt apology sometime later, I continued to want to hide every time I saw him. From that point on, I found myself downplaying my accomplishments. Shame had declared them null and void.

## Body Responses To Shame

My bodily responses to shame and condemnation can be just as intense as my responses to trauma (Brown, 2008). The amygdala, an almond-sized structure in the limbic system, processes emotional memory and threat. When I'm flooded with self-criticism and negativity, my body interprets these as danger signals.

In a way, self-criticism becomes a form of self-disclosure. What I cannot accept in myself, I attack. The words I once heard from others become my inner dialogue. I begin to treat myself the same way others once treated me, harshly, critically, punitively. I call myself names I absorbed long ago without even recognising the source: *"What's wrong with you?"* *"You're such an idiot."* My amygdala listens to all of it.

## Verbal Responses To Shame

Shame doesn't just stay inside, it spills out. I can turn the same language on others, especially those closest to me, my spouse, my children. What I condemn in them often mirrors what I most fear in myself. Rather than face the shame in my heart, I project it outward. I criticise and label them, as a way of managing my own internal discomfort.

It's a temptation from the enemy: rather than turning to God with my pain, I shift the focus. I might see a homeless person lying in their own urine and think, *"That would never happen to me. I'm not lazy like that."* But the voice is really for me. My amygdala hears it. I am still attacking myself.

## Mental And Emotional Responses To Shame

Children who grow up shamed often become adults who feel deeply unlovable and unacceptable. At its core, shame is a fear of disconnection, of not being worthy of belonging. And tragically, it becomes a self-fulfilling prophecy. If I believe I'm shameful, it's hard to trust anyone who loves me. And if someone *does* love me, I may not respect them, because I assume they must be wrong or misguided (Cozolino, 2013, p. 103).

Earlier, I spoke about Karen Horney's insight: to gain control over helplessness and avoid anxiety, we block our unmet needs by rejecting ourselves, just as our environment once rejected us (Horney, as cited in Teyber, 2005). I internalise the rejection and turn it into contempt. I tell myself, *"I'm too needy. I'm too much. I'm never enough."* And again, my amygdala listens. In doing so, I empower the enemy of my soul to reinforce the lie.

Shamed people often condemn themselves with lies the enemy implants into old emotional wounds. Some of these lies take the form of relentless internal dialogues. The right-hand column offers the antidote: truthful internal dialogues, how God sees me.

## Negative Internal Dialogues Are Not Our Own

The enemy uses every painful situation in our lives to implant his life-sapping lies through a broken relationship, a shaming environment, financial problems, addictions, physical flaws, wayward children, and so on. *"He [Satan] was a murderer from the beginning and does not stand in the truth, because there is no truth in him. When he tells a lie, he speaks his native language..."* (John 8:44, NIV). The enemy thrives on the distorted narratives we believe about ourselves and often whispers: *"You're not enough. You'll never be enough."*

But here's the good news: God's truth counters every lie. The lies that shame plants in our hearts can be uprooted, if we dare to believe God's better story. Truth shatters the enemy's lies, and it's not about us trying harder or striving to fix ourselves, it's about receiving the love, acceptance, and truth that God is offering us in Christ.

## The Power Of God's Truth

I've seen how God's truth has the power to reset shame narratives. In my own journey, I've had to confront the lies that said I wasn't enough, that I didn't deserve love or connection. These lies were deeply rooted in the pain of my past, but when I allowed God's truth to penetrate my heart, things began to shift.

For instance, when I finally faced the deep shame that I carried about not being good enough for my father's affection, I realized that God wasn't like my father. He didn't pull back in disappointment when I *"grew up."* Instead, God's love is relentless, unchanging, and expansive. I wasn't loved based on my performance or innocence; I was loved because of who I am in Christ, a beloved daughter, made in His image.

The more I meditated on this truth, the more I began to see myself differently, not as someone unworthy of affection, but as someone deeply loved by God. It wasn't an overnight transformation, but little by little, shame began to lose its grip. I learned that I didn't need to hide behind masks, trying to prove my worth or please others. I was already enough because of Christ (see Figure 6: *Negative and Truthful Dialogues*).

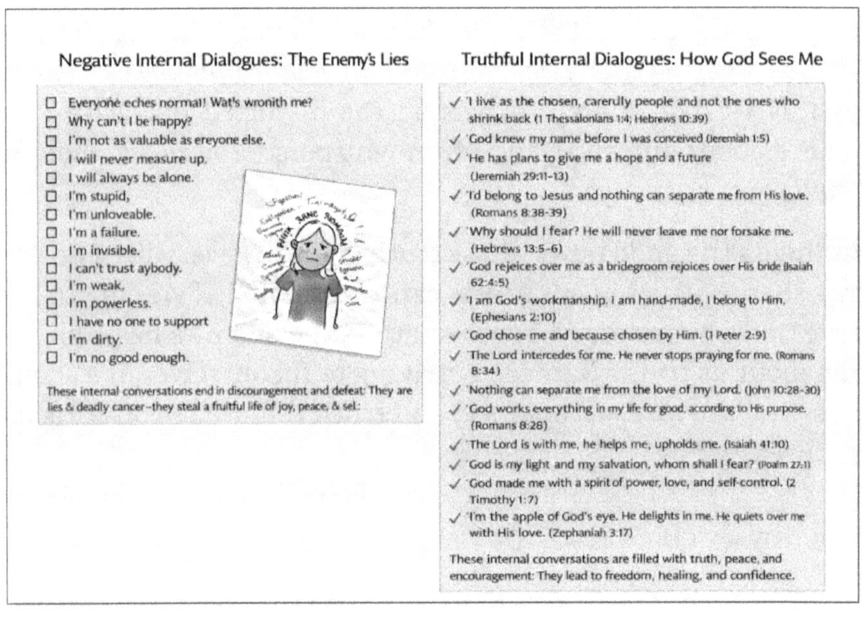


Figure 6. *Negative and Truthful Dialogues*

## Shame And The Need For Healing

Healing from shame doesn't mean pretending the past never happened or glossing over the hurt. It means acknowledging that the pain was real, but it doesn't define us. Healing comes when we stop trying to cover up the wound with false selves and start allowing God's grace to pour in. Healing comes when we accept that our past doesn't have to dictate our future and that, even in our brokenness, God is still doing something beautiful in us.

Remember the powerful verse in Isaiah 61 that says, *"He has sent me to bind up the brokenhearted, to proclaim freedom for the captives and release from darkness for the prisoners"* (Isaiah 61:1, NIV)? God is in the business of healing the brokenhearted. He binds up the wounds of shame and frees us from the darkness it traps us in. He invites us to step into His light and allow His love to wash over us, even in the places we feel most unlovable.

### Moving from Shame to Freedom

As we learn to reject the lies that shame tells us and embrace the truth of who God says we are, we move from living in a cage of shame to stepping into the freedom of God's love. This isn't just a one-time event, it's a journey. It's a process of unlearning the false narratives and embracing the new story God is writing over our lives.

As I continue to walk in this journey of healing, I'm learning to embrace the fullness of who I am in Christ. I no longer have to hide or perform to earn affection or approval. The more I lean into God's truth, the more I discover my true worth and identity in Him.

The good news of the Gospel is that shame doesn't have the final word. God does. His love speaks a better word over us, one that shatters the chains of shame and calls us to live freely and fully in His grace.

## Where Recovery Begins

Shame thrives in silence. But recovery begins in being seen. That's why, when those two little girls stepped into Jesus' arms in my vision, something shifted deep within me. He didn't rush them. He didn't force them to smile or behave. He just waited, arms open. He knew the way shame had silenced them. And He knew the way love would free them. Because when Jesus heals shame, He doesn't just tell us who we are, He shows us, by how He looks at us, how He touches the untouchable places, how He stays when others leave.

That is where recovery begins. In the gaze that does not look away. In the love that refuses to let shame have the final word.

## Closing Thoughts

So, let us walk in the freedom He offers, not just in moments of clarity, but in the daily courage it takes to bring our hidden selves into His healing light. This is the invitation of grace: to be seen, to be known, and still be called beloved.

But to truly receive this love, we must first understand what keeps us bound. Shame often takes root in childhood, especially when shaming experiences are left unrepaired by caregivers who are unable or unwilling to restore connection. These corrosive early moments shape the way we see ourselves, and how we see God. Instead of developing an internal sense of worth and security, we internalize the wounds of disconnection. We begin to believe that we are the problem. In response, we attack ourselves with criticism and perfectionism, or others with judgment and defensiveness. Without realizing it, we become agents of shame, both inwardly and outwardly.

For women, shame often takes the form of relentless pressure to meet impossible internal standards. For men, it can centre around the fear of inadequacy, disrespect, or the ridicule of their manhood. No matter how it manifests, shame isolates and erodes our sense of belovedness. It doesn't just distort our view of self; it blinds us to the truth of how God sees us.

Shame and condemnation are energy-draining addictions to unbelief. They infect every part of our lives, stealing vitality, clouding joy, and distorting love. One of the cruellest aspects of shame is its vagueness, there's often no specific issue to resolve, no clear moment to fix. It simply is, lingering like a heavy fog in the soul.

And make no mistake: the author of shame is Satan. He plants deceptive lies in the soil of our pain, and they take root, growing into internal dialogues that sound like truth but are far from it. Lies that say we are unworthy, unlovable, or beyond repair. But these are not God's words. God never intended His children to live as prisoners of shame. His truth tells a different story, one of worth, freedom, and grace.

In the next chapter, *The Heavy Heart of Shame*, we'll take a deeper look at how shame embeds itself in the soul: how it forms, how it lingers, and how it can be unmasked. Because if shame is the fog that clouds our view, then truth is the light that gently burns it away. And as that light begins to break through, we find that we were never too far gone. We were always seen. Always loved. Always held.

---

## Declarations

I declare and renounce shame and the lie that says I am bad, dirty, ugly, stupid, worthless, or damaged.

I declare the Truth that Jesus died for my sins and that I am forgiven, washed, cleansed, justified, and accepted.

---

## Prayer

*Yes, Lord, I have to die - with you, through you, and in you - and thus become ready to recognize you when you appear to me in your resurrection. There is so much in me that needs to die: false attachments, greed and anger, impatience and stinginess.*

*O Lord, I am self-centred, concerned about myself, my career, my future, my name and fame.*

*Often, I even feel that I use you to my own advantage.*

*Yes, Lord, I know it is true. I know that often I have spoken about you, written about you, and acted in your name for my own glory and success. Your name has not led me to persecution, oppression, or rejection. Your name has brought me rewards! I see clearly how little I have died with you, really gone your way and been faithful to it.*

*O Lord, make this...season different from the other ones. Let me find you again. Amen.*
(Henri Nouwen, 2013, *A Cry for Mercy*)

---

## Reflection Questions

1. How did shame develop in your childhood?
2. How have shaming experiences affected your ability to form an authentic view of yourself?
3. What role did the inability or unwillingness of a parent to repair play in the development of your shame?
4. How does shame prevent you from seeing yourslef through God's eyes and from experiencing true self-worth?
5. In what ways do you respond to shame by attacking yourself and others with criticism and negativity?
6. In what ways do Satan's lies manifest as negative internal dialogues, and how do these prevent you from developing an authentic view of how God sees you?

## Journal Prompt

What is one lie shame has told you about yourself, and what might God's truth be instead?
Let your pen move without censoring. See what flows out.

# CHAPTER 17

## *Unpacking the Weight of Shame*

---

*"To be yourself in a world that is constantly trying to make you something else is the greatest accomplishment." ~ Ralph Waldo Emerson*

*"To embrace and love who we are, we have to reclaim and reconnect with the parts of ourselves we've orphaned over the years." ~ Brené Brown, Rising Strong*

*"Let your love, God, shape my life." ~ Psalm 119:41 (MSG)*

---

### When Being Becomes The Burden

Shame is a heavy burden, but unlike physical weight, it doesn't show on the outside. It hides beneath competence, kindness, success, even faith. It whispers lies about our worth and warps our identity. Unlike guilt, which tells us we've done something wrong, shame tells us *we are* something wrong. It doesn't ask for change; it demands concealment. And over time, that concealment costs us our wholeness, our voice, even our capacity to receive love.

This chapter explores the subtle and suffocating grip of shame, how it begins, how it embeds itself into our thoughts, relationships, and spirituality, and how, through grace, it can begin to lift. To unpack shame is to confront the false agreements we've made about ourselves and God, to grieve what was lost, and to risk stepping into the truth: that we are deeply loved, even in our most vulnerable places.

## The Incident

An incident with my granddaughter shook me deeply, one I'll carry with me for a long time. It was late in the day, after preschool, ballet, and the park, our usual rhythm. Part of our routine was always walking from ballet to the ice cream shop, where we'd deliberate over the best flavour. She'd take forever to decide, but when we finally made our choices, we'd always share a taste. Sometimes, she'd even decide mine tasted better and take mine, leaving me with hers.

On this particular day, her preschool friend joined us at the park. The two of them climbed onto the round rope swing, twisting and contorting themselves as Poppy propelled them higher and higher. It was carefree joy, until it was disrupted. There was another child on the swing, an adult-child with developmental impairments, who suddenly became distressed and vomited on my granddaughter's friend. The scene was chaotic, with loud crying filling the park. My granddaughter, witnessing the tragedy unfold, held it all in for the sake of her friend.

I know transitions are hard for four- and five-year-olds. My granddaughter is no exception. She always resists leaving the park and today was no different. We tried to make it a game, challenging her to race us to the car. But instead of running, she veered off toward the bike rack, climbing onto the bar for a swing of her own. I waited patiently, as I often do. Then, with a resounding thud, she fell. It wasn't a severe fall, but the emotional impact was immense, triggering a wave of frustration and hurt she'd been holding onto all day.

Her big feelings took over. I tried to comfort her, but she screamed, “Go away.” The words stung. There was no warning, no sign that the moment would shift from calm to intense so suddenly. I sat beside her, close enough to keep her safe but far enough to give her space.

I tried everything, the usual tactics. I bribed her with ice cream, threatened to take away privileges, even tried to reason with her. But nothing worked. Each offer seemed to bounce off her, and the more I pushed, the more she dug in her heels. When I attempted to lift her into the car, she bolted. My heart raced with fear, terrified she'd run straight into the busy street. The thought of her in danger, the loss of control, it took me right to the edge.

After a few long moments, she slowed, sitting beside the car. Her defiance was still there, but her energy shifted. She wasn't in full meltdown anymore, but the power struggle had clearly taken its toll. When it came time to get in the car, she chose to enter from the front seat, not the back as usual, asserting her control over the moment. In her quiet, determined way, she had won the power struggle. And I was left to process the aftermath.

## The Aftermath

I knew her reaction wasn't about me, not really. It was about something deeper. And in that moment, I realized that her big emotions were mirrors to the unresolved wounds in me. Children are masters at reflecting our unhealed parts, aren't they? It's humbling to realize how much of what we feel and how we respond is deeply intertwined with our own unresolved issues.

Writing helps me process these moments. Typing away allows me to make sense of the complex emotions I was feeling, still feeling, even four days later. It wasn't just the incident that mattered; it was what it stirred within me. I began to recognize how fear had become a constant companion in my relationship with my granddaughter. Fear of failing her, fear of not knowing how to help her. It was always there, lurking beneath the surface. But that day, it wasn't just any fear. It felt like a flashback, like a trigger from a time when I'd felt completely powerless, out of control.

When that happened, my reaction wasn't grounded. I slipped into survival mode. My body flooded with stress hormones, and my mind checked out. Instead of staying calm, I tried to control everything around me. I manipulated the situation, bribing, threatening, anything to make her stop feeling so much. Anything to calm my own emotional storm.

But that's the thing about triggers, they aren't rational. When I'm triggered, my body reacts before my mind can catch up. It's emotional, physiological, and everything in between. In that moment, I lost my centre. I lost the ability to stay present. Instead of holding boundaries, I was trying to calm my own inner chaos.

## The Convergence

In the aftermath of the park incident, I found myself unravelling. I was irritable, snapping at my husband, retreating into myself. Despite the external calm, so much was happening inside me. My morning devotions became a quiet refuge, a space where I could wrestle with the emotions stirred by the events of the day. I prayed, asking God to heal the desolate parts of me, the parts that had been dried out by fear and unprocessed pain.

Around this time, my husband and I were participating in a marriage course. One of the key discussions cantered on the dynamics between a husband and wife, with the wife feeling like she was *"too much"* and the husband feeling *"not enough."* This conversation highlighted something my husband hadn't realized before: the one who emotionally withdraws in a relationship often holds the power. By controlling when and how they engage, they control the level of connection.

The next morning, my husband came to me, tears in his eyes. He apologized for withdrawing, for controlling the relationship. It was a moment of revelation for him. He'd always believed his emotional distance was about self-protection, but now he saw it differently. Something deep inside me shifted in that moment. I felt the park incident, the emotions I was grappling with, and the work I was doing in counselling all coming together in a way I hadn't anticipated.

## The Aftermath And Revelation

The next few days after the park incident were tough. Though the external calm had returned, I was far from settled. I was irritable, snapping at my husband, withdrawing into myself. A lot was happening inside me, and I didn't have the energy to explain it all. My thoughts felt like a tangled mess, and my emotions were on overdrive. It wasn't just about what had happened with my granddaughter, but the years of unprocessed feelings, the old wounds that were now coming to the surface.

In the quiet moments, I found solace in my morning devotions. I needed space to process, to allow God to speak into the mess of my emotions. I prayed, asking God to meet me in my brokenness, to heal those parts of me that felt so dry and distant. I needed His presence to soothe the sharp edges of my heart, the places where shame had settled for far too long.

During that time, my husband and I were engaged in a marriage course. One of the key discussions centred on a common dynamic between couples: the wife feeling like she's *"too much"* and the husband feeling like he's *"not enough."* It was a deep conversation that my husband hadn't realized he needed to hear. In it, I saw how my emotional withdrawal and his attempts to control our relationship had impacted us both. He shared his realization that his emotional distance was a way of protecting himself, but it also meant he was withdrawing from me, something I had never fully recognized until now.

The morning after the course, he came to me with tears in his eyes. He apologized for withdrawing, for not being more emotionally present. It was a significant moment for him, and I felt the weight of it. I knew, deep down, that his apology wasn't just for our marriage, it was a release from the fear and shame that had held both of us captive for so long.

## Facing Shame: A Generational Struggle

As I sat with this revelation, I began to see something bigger at play. Shame had woven itself through my life in ways I hadn't fully understood. It was always there, lurking beneath the surface, influencing my actions, my reactions, and the way I viewed myself. Shame made me feel like I was "too much", that my emotions were too intense, too out of control, too dangerous. It made me believe I wasn't worthy of love or understanding unless I kept those emotions in check, buried deep inside.

It wasn't just something I carried alone. It was a generational curse, passed down through the families we were born into. In my own upbringing, emotions were something to be feared, controlled, hidden away. Vulnerability was a weakness. When my feelings became too big, too loud, I was taught to push them down. Cry alone. Don't show weakness. Don't be too much. And so, I carried that with me, into my marriage, into my relationships, into my role as a mother and a grandmother.

The shame was compounded by the church, a place where I had hoped for healing but often found more condemnation. We were taught to suppress our emotions in the name of *"joy and peace."* Grief, anger, sadness, these were things to be avoided, not expressed. Even now, as I think about my own experience, I can't help but wonder how many people have internalized that message. How many of us have learned to hide our true selves, believing that God only wants our happiness, our polished perfection?

But now, as I look at my granddaughter, I see something different. I see a child who feels deeply and unapologetically. She isn't ashamed of her emotions. She lets them flow freely, and in doing so, she teaches me something I've forgotten. It's okay to feel, even the hard things. It's okay to express what's inside without fear of judgment or rejection.

## Healing The Wounds Of Shame

In the quiet moments, I'm beginning to realize that my own big emotions, once something I tried to suppress, are not the enemy. They're part of me. They're part of what it means to be human, to be alive, to be fully present in the world. I don't need to hide them. I don't need to apologize for feeling deeply.

Shame has had its grip on me for so long. But now, I'm learning to let go of it. I'm learning that I don't have to be defined by it. I don't have to live in fear of my emotions or the reactions they might provoke in others. I'm starting to believe that, maybe for the first time in my life, I am enough as I am, emotions and all.

And as I journey through this, I'm learning to embrace the parts of me that I've long hidden away. I'm asking God to heal those broken places, to meet me in my pain and show me the way forward. Because the truth is, I can't heal on my own. I need Him to do the work that I can't do. And in that healing, I'm finding peace. Not a peace that comes from avoiding the mess of emotions, but a peace that comes from knowing that God sees me, loves me, and calls me His own, just as I am.

## Trapped In A Cycle Of Shame

Shame ensnares us in a perpetual cycle of self-loathing or condemnation, draining our energy and becoming an integral part of our existence. To bolster our fragile sense of security, we often resort to projecting strength, as exemplified by Barry's sense of inadequacy, which he covers with an exaggerated sense of responsibility. Remember how Genesis 3:7 aptly states, "*Then the eyes of both of them were opened, and they realized they were naked; so they sewed fig leaves together and made coverings for themselves.*" Consequently, shame becomes a rigid adherence to erroneous beliefs about ourselves and others, leaving no room for compromise. While we were born with inherent freedom, we often find ourselves ensnared in oppressive chains (Rousseau, cited in Kelman, 2009).

Regrettably, the pervasive nature of shame often leads us to perpetuate self-destructive patterns. It can manifest in various ways, anger, depression, control, judgment, criticism, withdrawal, people-pleasing, perfectionism, striving, self-deception, or a lack of initiative. These behaviours reinforce shame and hinder our personal growth and well-being.

## How Shame Becomes A Lifestyle

Madame Curie, the Polish French physicist, chemist, and pioneering figure in the field of radioactivity, is a striking example of someone addressing her insecurities with unwavering strength. As the first female professor at the Sorbonne and the first person to win two Nobel Prizes in different sciences, she became renowned not only for her discoveries but also for her resilience. Yet, her personal life reveals a tragic element of denial. One account of her life reads:

> *"Today I was reading about Madame Curie: She must have known she suffered from radiation sickness her body bombarded for years by the element she had purified. It seems she denied to the end the source of the cataracts on her eyes the cracked and suppurating skin of her finger-ends till she could no longer hold a test-tube or a pencil. She died a famous woman denying her wounds*

*denying her wounds came from the same source as her power" (Rich, Gelphi & Gelphi, 1993, p. 73).*

Madame Curie's life exemplifies a kind of self-punishing denial, where the progression of shame from a significant wound gradually morphs into a lifestyle (see *Figure 7. The Progression of Shame*).

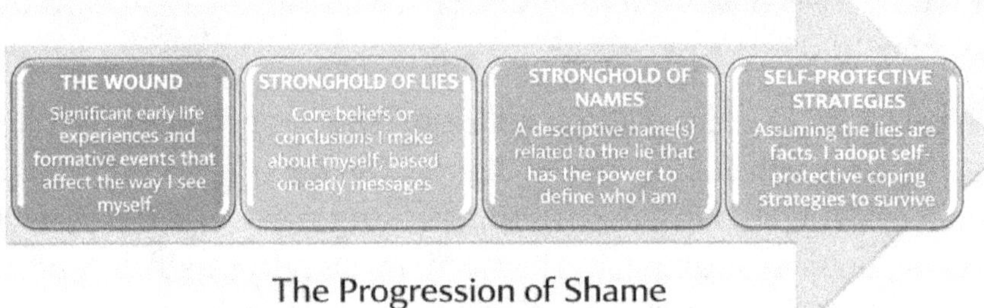


Figure 7. *The Progression of Shame*

It's crucial to note that shame is not inherently shameful. As Anaïs Nin (n.d.) wisely stated, *"Shame is the lie someone tells you about yourself."* Instead of dwelling in shame, we should cultivate an appreciation for the survival mechanisms that have protected us. Acknowledging the value of these defences allows us to develop greater empathy and understanding for others' self-protective behaviours.

Healing arises when we take responsibility for our negative responses, seek repentance, and extend forgiveness to ourselves and others. Transitioning to healthier coping mechanisms requires time, and self-compassion is essential in this process. Moreover, there may be reluctance to abandon self-protective strategies unless we identify alternative ways to cope. Often, we hold deeply ingrained beliefs in the lies planted by the enemy in our wounds. Shame prevents us from experiencing positive input because we believe the enemy's lies.

## Bringing Shame Into The Light

Shame is a master of disguise. It hides behind unhealthy behaviours, emotional reactivity, and broken relationships. It isolates us from others and even from ourselves. And yet, if we want to restore true connection, with God, with others, and within our own hearts, we must dare to bring our shame out of hiding (Brown, 2007, p. 276; 2012, p. 110).

But this is no easy invitation. Why would we willingly revisit our shame, knowing it might stir up old wounds or painful memories? Doesn't reflection risk falling into a self-absorbed trap, or even divert us from spiritual maturity?

## The Illusion Of Self-Sufficiency

The answer is both simple and deeply spiritual: when we refuse to face our shame, we risk becoming falsely independent. We start to believe that we are in control, that we can manage life on our own terms, that we must be our own masters. But self-sufficiency is an illusion, it fosters either confusion or quiet arrogance. Even Jesus asked the man who had been sick for thirty-eight years, *"Do you want to get well?"* (John 5:6). It's a piercing question. Healing requires change, and change requires courage. Are we truly seeking transformation, or just venting our frustrations? Are we ready to own our shame, or do we still find comfort in blaming others?

Taking responsibility for our shame is the beginning of healing (Seamands, 2015). When we are willing to acknowledge it, not only before God, but also with someone we trust, its grip begins to loosen. We find, paradoxically, that vulnerability leads to strength. And as we learn to offer this honesty to others, we become safe spaces where healing can happen.

## Listening To The Language Of Emotions

As a trauma counsellor and someone who once wrestled with depression, I've learned that the mind can spiral quickly, dragging us into darker places. Our thoughts try hard to make sense of our pain, but they don't always tell the truth. Sometimes we need to stop the mental noise and listen more deeply to the quiet cry of the heart.

Emotions are the soul's language. They don't lie. Like my granddaughter's cries when she's tired or hungry, our emotions are signposts that reveal our needs and desires. They help us interpret our internal world, not as enemies to suppress, but as messengers to receive with curiosity and grace. When we learn to listen to our shame, we begin to heal.

## Healing Through Sharing Shame With God

One of the most powerful pathways to healing is sharing our shame with God. It may feel counterintuitive, after all, isn't shame the very thing that makes us want to hide from Him? And yet, when we confess, when we allow ourselves to be seen and known, we open the door to transformation. Repentance isn't about grovelling in guilt, it's about returning to love. It helps us name the harm we've done to others, to ourselves, and even to our image of God.

John Calvin once said that true wisdom consists in knowing God and knowing ourselves (Calhoun, 2005, p. 23). Without self-awareness, we cannot truly know the One in whose image we were made. And it turns out that this kind of confession doesn't only heal us emotionally, it can even improve our physical health. Research has shown that confiding in safe people (and in God) can strengthen our cardiovascular system (Uchino et al., 1996). The body keeps the score, but so does the heart. And healing comes when we're no longer alone with our shame.

This is not just about emotional relief, it's about a deep, spiritual assurance. The shame of sin, of separation, of not being enough, is replaced by the honour of being called beloved. We are no longer defined by our failures, our trauma, or the judgments of others. We are defined by grace. To believe in Jesus is to embrace the identity God gives: chosen, accepted, and secure. And in that identity, shame no longer has the final word.

## Understanding The Truth About Shame

God uses the truth about shame to heal us. To experience this healing, we must explore how we view God and uncover the lies the enemy has planted in our shame. Here is the truth of what God says about shame:

- **Psalm 25:3**: *"No one who hopes in you will ever be put to shame..."*
- **Psalm 31:1**: *"In you, Lord, I have taken refuge; let me never be put to shame; deliver me in your righteousness."*
- **Romans 5:5**: *"And hope does not put us to shame, because God's love has been poured out into our hearts through the Holy Spirit, who has been given to us."*
- **Romans 10:11**: *"As Scripture says, 'Anyone who believes in him will never be put to shame.'"*
- **Jude 1:24**: *"To him who is able to keep you from stumbling and to present you before his glorious presence without fault and with great joy..."*

One of the foundations of emotional healing is coming to deeply know that God loves, forgives, and accepts us. The Apostle Paul, who knew shame and condemnation intimately, was able to grasp God's perspective. Remember that Paul was a murderer of Christians. In fact, when he met Jesus, he was on his way to commit murder. Paul could have been consumed by shame and self-condemnation, but instead, he chose to focus on God's grace.

He shared that, though he was not perfect, he was pressing forward, reaching out to Christ, who had reached out to him (Philippians 3:12-14). Paul understood that he had left his past behind and was focused on the goal: Jesus. He moved forward and would not stop.

When we carry the burden of shame, we hinder the healing process. Shame prevents us from fully trusting in the heart of Jesus. Many of God's children don't experience the fullness of His grace, remaining unable to feel deeply loved and known by Him. This forfeits the power of God in our lives, keeping us in bondage to the enemy. The enemy's goal is to hold us captive, but Matthew West (2012), in his song *Hello, My Name Is*, powerfully depicts this battle:

> *"Hello, my name is regret*
> *I'm pretty sure we have met*
> *Every single day of your life*
> *I'm the whisper inside*
> *Won't let you forget*
> *Hello, my name is defeat*
> *I know you recognize me*
> *Just when you think you can win*
> *I'll drag you right back down again*
> *'Til you've lost all belief*
> *These are the voices,*
> *these are the lies*
> *And I have believed them,*
> *for the very last time."*

Yet God knows us intimately and affirms, *"Before I formed you in the womb I knew you, before you were born I set you apart..."* (Jeremiah 1:5). We were hand-crafted by the Creator of the universe. As 2 Corinthians 5:17 declares, *"Therefore, if anyone is in Christ, he is a new creation: the old has gone, the new has come."* So, what does it mean to be a new creation in Christ Jesus?

Shame and condemnation are focused on us, but grace is about Jesus, who died and rose again to set us free. Paul was a new creation in Christ, and he was not tormented by shame and condemnation because he was able to let go of the past and focus on his future in Christ. By embracing the truth of our new identity in Christ, we can thwart the enemy's lies.

## Closing Thoughts

In the last chapter, we began to unpack the heavy heart of shame, how it forms, how it clings to us, and how it distorts the truth of who we are. We named its roots in early wounds and unmet needs, exposed the lies it whispers, and reflected on how shame can blind us to the grace of God. But as we begin to loosen shame's grip, another layer of healing invites us forward: the power of story.

As we've explored, understanding and confronting shame is only the first step in our healing journey. Recognizing the truth of our identity in Christ and learning to rest in God's unchanging love can begin to shift the deep narratives of unworthiness that shame writes into our souls. But healing often requires us to go even deeper, to step into the stories that shape us and allow them to be seen, re-examined, and reinterpreted through the lens of grace.

We are storied people. And shame, perhaps more than any other emotion, is embedded in the stories we carry, both spoken and unspoken. Stories of failure. Rejection. Disconnection. Silence. But shame does not only live in our individual stories, but it is also part of the collective human experience. And so is redemption.

The Bible, in its rich tapestry of characters and events, offers us a mirror. It's filled with men and women who stumbled, who hid, who carried the unbearable weight of shame, and who, in their brokenness, encountered the mercy of God. These are not just ancient accounts; they are echoes of our own struggles. When we see ourselves in their stories, we also begin to see how

God enters into the mess, covering shame with compassion and turning wounds into windows of grace.

In the next chapter, *Stories of Shame: Finding Freedom in Our Narratives*, we'll explore the stories of Adam and Eve, Judas, Peter, and others, people who wrestled with the weight of shame. Some, like Peter, were met by a God who restored and redeemed their failure. Others, like Judas, could not see a path beyond their shame and turned away. Each story invites us to reflect on our own response to shame, whether we hide, despair, or run toward grace. These narratives don't just reveal the human struggle; they reveal the heart of a God who moves toward us in our brokenness, offering healing, if we will receive it. Their journeys offer us hope that even in our most shame-filled moments, God moves toward us with tenderness, not condemnation.

So let us walk into these stories with open hearts, not just as readers, but as fellow travellers. Let us allow these sacred narratives to speak into our own, revealing the God who sees us, knows us, and lovingly rewrites the ending.

---

## Declarations

I declare that God makes all grace abound toward me so that I always have all sufficiency and an abundance for every good work.

I declare that God has a better covering for me than shame and condemnation. As I seek God, I am covered under His wings and hidden in the secret place of His tent (Psalm 91:1-4; 27:5) with coverings that are thick, warm, and protective.

I declare that God clothes me in clean robes, even when Satan accuses me before God's throne (Zechariah 3).

I declare that God's coverings are indications of honour, placing favour and protection on my unworthiness.

---

## Prayer

If you are ready, pray this prayer:

*Satan, I bind you in the powerful name of Jesus from placing thoughts of shame and condemnation into my mind. When the thoughts come, I will remind you that I belong to Jesus and He has forgiven me though His shed blood on the cross for me. He never condemns me. Jesus, I am sorry for believing the enemy's lies. Your voice is always loving and truthful. Thank You that You never condemn me. Thank You that You totally and completely accept me because the blood of Jesus covers me and makes me acceptable to You. Help me live in the light of this truth. In Jesus name. Amen.*

---

## Reflection Questions

1. Why is an authentic view of both God and the self, crucial for healing from past wounds and overcoming your shame?
2. How does healing from your shame lead to self-acceptance, allowing you to see yourself through God's eyes?
3. How does shaming affect your identity and self-condemnation?
4. How does shame lose power when you embrace God's perspective?
5. How does changing your false self-images to authenticity lead to freedom and life?
6. What does it mean to be aware of yourself as *"the clay in the potter's hands,"* and how can you remain soft and

sensitive to God's shaping?

7. How do you identify and confront the lies perpetuated by the enemy through past wounds?
8. How can you resist the devil, causing him to flee (as instructed in James 4:7)?
9. How are strongholds in your life destroyed in the battle against the enemy seeking your destruction?

---

## Journal Prompt

Reflect on a time when you felt overwhelmed by shame. What lies were you believing in that moment, and how can you replace them with the truth of your identity in Christ?
Let your pen move without censoring. See what flows out.

# CHAPTER 18

## Rewriting Shame

---

*"She remembered the story from her childhood, about Adam and Eve in the garden, and the talking snake. Even as a little girl she had said - to the consternation of her family - What kind of idiot was Eve, to believe a snake? But now she understood, for she had heard the voice of the snake and had watched as a wise and powerful man had fallen under its spell. Eat the fruit and you can have the desires of your heart. It's not evil, it's noble and good. You'll be praised for it. And it's delicious." ~ Orson Scott Card, Shadow of the Hegemon*

*"Have you heard of the most evil things done by people in their lifetime? They have coveted men's wives, killed hundreds of Christians and sold their best friend's life away for just a few coins. Isn't it interesting that they were God's chosen in the bible? - Saul, Judas & King David." ~ Shannon L. Alder*

*"Peter denied Jesus; Judas betrayed Jesus. The bad news was that both of them fell off the track and were both filled with regrets, remorse and anguish for their mischievous behaviours. However it was only Peter who chose to rise again after falling! Judas chose to end it with suicide! If you fall, you can rise again!" ~ Israelmore Ay-*

*ivor, The Great Hand Book of Quotes*

---

## From Hiding To Healing

Shame is one of the oldest human experiences. It isolates us, silences us, and convinces us we are beyond repair. But the story of shame doesn't have to end in hiding. It can be rewritten. Not through perfection or performance, but through truth, grace, and the courage to face what we fear most about ourselves.

The Bible provides profound stories about shame, some heart-breaking, others deeply redemptive. In the garden of Eden, we see shame's origin in Adam and Eve's hiding. In Judas, we witness how shame, when left to fester in isolation, leads to despair. And in Peter, we see the difference that grace makes, how even deep failure can be transformed by love and restored identity.

This chapter explores these three stories and invites us to reflect on our own. What if shame is not the final word? What if the God who clothed Adam and Eve, wept for Judas, and restored Peter, is writing a new ending for us too?

## The First Emotion: Shame

In the beginning, shame was not part of God's creation. Genesis 2:25 tells us, *"And they were both naked, the man and his wife, and they were not ashamed."* In the Garden of Eden, Adam and Eve lived in the pure delight of God's presence. They knew no shame, but once they ate from the tree of knowledge, everything changed. They realized their nakedness and covered themselves with fig leaves, marking the entrance of shame into the human experience. Their sin led them to hide from each other, and from God.

The consequence? The expulsion from paradise, and from that moment on, shame became a constant companion. It's a haunting truth: since that time, humanity has hidden behind fig leaves, false identities, striving to cover our shame.

## Judas

Judas Iscariot's story is a tragic study in shame's destructive power. Judas, one of Jesus's closest disciples, led a group of soldiers to the Garden of Gethsemane to betray Jesus with a kiss. The act itself was shameful, but what followed was even worse. Upon realizing the enormity of his actions, Judas felt deep remorse. He tried to undo his betrayal, returning the thirty pieces of silver he had received. But when the chief priests and elders rejected his attempt at restitution, Judas was left alone with his guilt and despair.

His remorse, while real, did not lead to repentance. He couldn't reconcile his actions with God's forgiveness. Instead, he chose the darkness of suicide, further sealing his sense of rejection and hopelessness. Judas's inability to seek forgiveness led to a tragic end, a stark reminder of the power of unresolved shame.

I see part of myself in Judas. There have been times when I couldn't find hope in my own shame. Like Judas, I felt overwhelmed by regret, unable to grasp the truth of God's forgiveness. At one point, this led me to consider taking my own life, as I thought there was no way out. But God's mercy met me in my darkness.

## Peter

Peter's story offers a stark contrast to Judas's. After denying Jesus three times, Peter's heart was shattered with shame. Yet, his response to shame was not despair, but humility and repentance. On the night of Jesus's arrest, Peter, in a moment of fear, denied knowing Jesus three times, just as Jesus had predicted. When the rooster crowed, Peter remembered Jesus's words and felt profound grief. Luke 22:62 tells us, *"And he went outside and wept bitterly."* He had failed his Lord, and his shame was overwhelming.

Peter, crushed by the weight of his failure, decided to return to fishing, the life he knew before Jesus called him. But Jesus wasn't done with Peter. On the shore, Jesus called to him, inviting him to restore what had been broken. In a deeply symbolic moment, Jesus asked Peter three times if he loved Him, providing Peter with an opportunity to undo his three denials. Peter, broken and repentant, responded each time with a deep affirmation of his love for Jesus. Jesus forgave him, and Peter's restoration was complete. Jesus even entrusted him with the care of His flock: *"Feed my sheep"* (John 21:15-17).

Peter's response to shame, his repentance, his turning back to Jesus, led to his restoration, not just spiritually but in his calling. His story is a testimony to the grace that always pursues us, even when we fail. It's a reminder that God's forgiveness is greater than any shame we carry, and that He calls us to a life of purpose, even after we've stumbled.

Romans 8:1 speaks so clearly to those of us who struggle with shame: *"There is now no condemnation for those who are in Christ Jesus."* Peter's story, like God's promise, offers comfort to me: no matter how deeply I've failed, God's love is steadfast, and His forgiveness is sure.

## The Redemption Of Shame: Empathy And Vulnerability

Peter's restoration is not only a story of grace, but also a story of how vulnerability creates space for healing and intimacy. Around the charcoal fire, Jesus doesn't shame Peter, nor does He rehash the failure. Instead, He offers Peter a chance to be seen, not just as a man who failed, but as one who still longs to love and follow. Jesus meets Peter in the precise place of his shame, not to condemn but to restore.

This moment is deeply empathetic. Jesus doesn't correct Peter with a theological lecture. He doesn't demand an apology. He simply asks a question: *"Do you love me?"* three times, each echoing one of Peter's denials. The repetition isn't for punishment. It's for healing. It is Jesus saying, *"I know you, and I still want you."* This is what empathy looks like: seeing someone in their most broken state and staying present. Not fixing. Not withdrawing. Just staying.

In Peter's vulnerability, his willingness to answer Jesus honestly, his willingness to feel and not defend or explain away, restoration begins. Shame makes us want to hide, like Adam and Eve did in the garden. But vulnerability invites us to step into the light, even trembling, even unsure. It opens the door for love to reach us in our most wounded places.

In contrast, Judas never opens himself to this kind of vulnerable encounter. He isolates. He hides in his remorse. His shame festers alone. We don't know what might have happened if Judas had gone to Jesus. But we do know that repentance, reconciliation, and restoration are always possible when we allow ourselves to be known, when we risk vulnerability in the presence of compassion.

I think that's what has saved me too. When shame drove me to the brink, it wasn't someone fixing me that helped, it was being met with empathy. A friend who didn't try to correct me. A counsellor who didn't recoil from my story. My husband who didn't walk away when I confessed the depth of my pain. Their steady presence reminded me of God's. Each time I chose to speak honestly, to risk being vulnerable, I cracked open the door just wide enough for grace to come through.

When I read Peter's story, I see myself, not only in his failure but in his longing. I want to be loved like that. I want to be called back from shame and entrusted again with purpose. And I want to offer that same love to others. I want to become the kind of person who doesn't look away when others are weeping by the fire of their own failure.

Empathy is the antidote to shame. Vulnerability is the doorway to redemption. And Jesus, the One who knows us fully and loves us still, invites us into both. Romans 8:1 continues to speak healing to my heart: *"There is now no condemnation for those who are in Christ Jesus."* No condemnation. Not even for the parts of us that still ache. Not even for the parts that tremble when we tell the truth.

Jesus doesn't flinch from our wounds. He draws closer.

## Closing Thoughts

Shame, as we've seen, is a master of disguise. It convinces us we are unworthy, unlovable, and irredeemable. It echoes the lies we've absorbed from past wounds and embeds them deep in our identity. But shame begins to lose its grip when we allow ourselves to be seen, first by God, then by others, and finally, by ourselves through the lens of God's truth.

Understanding both God's perspective and our own is essential for healing. As long as we view ourselves through the distorted lens of shame, we cannot step into the freedom and fullness of life God intends for us. But when we dare to look again, when we expose shame to the light and let grace reinterpret our story, our false self-image begins to give way to authenticity. We stop hiding behind perfectionism, performance, or silence. Instead, we begin to live out of who we truly are: *Beloved, chosen, and called.*

Thomas Green said it beautifully: *"Only those fully secure in their love can live fully in the present. Only those who've forgotten themselves, who float free, can bless the wind and the wave."* When we are secure in God's love, we stop striving to be enough. We rest in the truth that we already are, because He is enough. Slowly, we become vessels through which love flows freely. Mouldable. Surrendered. Shaped by love rather than fear.

But we must not forget, this healing journey is not only emotional, it is spiritual. There is an enemy of our soul who relentlessly works to distort the truth of who we are. The shame we carry is not merely psychological, it is rooted in spiritual warfare. The whispers of accusation: *You're too broken. You'll never change. You're beyond grace,* are not simply internal; they are strategies of a deeper, darker battle.

Yet Jesus has given us authority to resist. He invites us to stand firm, not in our strength but in His. Courage makes its entrance when we bring our wounds into the light, when we choose truth over lies, and when we remember that love is stronger than shame.

In my next book in this journey, *Exploring the Roots of Heartache,* we begin to uncover the deeper layers of emotional pain that often lie buried beneath the surface. These wounds are not always visible, but they are deeply felt. They shape our longings, influence our relationships, and cloud our experience of God and self. Let's continue this journey not with fear, but with courage, and the quiet trust that even in our deepest ache, God is already drawing near.

---

## Declarations

I declare that I am no longer defined by shame or past wounds. My identity is rooted in Christ, who calls me beloved, chosen, and whole.

I declare that the lies of the enemy have no authority over me. I stand in the truth of God's Word and resist every accusation with the shield of faith.

I declare that I am being transformed by the renewing of my mind. Old patterns, false beliefs, and toxic thoughts are being replaced by God's truth and love.

I declare that I am clay in the hands of the Potter, soft, surrendered, and open to the healing touch of my Creator.

---

## Prayer

*Lord,*
*You see every wound, every place in my heart that still aches with shame or fear. Thank You that You do not turn away but draw near with gentleness and truth. Help me to see myself through Your eyes, beloved, redeemed, and made whole. Where lies have taken root, plant Your truth. Where shame has silenced me, speak Your love louder. I surrender my heart into Your hands, Potter of my soul. Shape me into someone who lives free, fully present, and deeply rooted in Your grace. In Jesus' name, Amen.*

---

## Reflection Questions

1. When have I most felt the weight of shame, and what message did it communicate about my worth?
2. How have past wounds shaped the way I see myself, and are those perceptions aligned with how God sees me?
3. In what areas of my life do I still struggle to receive God's love or believe I am enough?
4. What would it look like for me to live from a place of authenticity and security in God's love?

---

## Journal Prompt

Take a moment to write a letter to your younger self, the part of you that first felt the sting of shame. What do you want them to know now about who they are, how deeply they are loved, and how God sees them? As you write, invite the Holy Spirit to guide your words with compassion and truth.

# ACKNOWLEDGEMENTS

A famous musician once said, *"I don't write songs, they write me."* Once I began this book, the ideas and words flowed freely and effortlessly from a deep, spiritual place in me, for which I thank God. Writing a book around the stories in my life has been a surreal process, more rewarding than I could have imagined. Many special people have been there across the years, speaking healing into my life, even though they may not have known it. I am deeply indebted to Larry Crabb, Dan Allender, Charles Swindoll, John Webb, Ruth Morgan, Paula D'Arcy, and John Eldridge. You opened my heart and awakened me to wrestle with deep-rooted issues in need of healing.

I am also honoured to be a part of a global community. Thank you for embracing me and allowing me to serve you. I thank my lifelong friends in Sri Lanka, India, and Europe for showing up at our workshops and teaching me that there is beauty and hope even in the darkest places. The world is a better place because of you.

I am also grateful to be part of my Australian community. To the couples who believed in us enough to encourage us to write and present our first marriage weekend in the late '80s, who would have known it would become global? To those in my church who have supported and faithfully prayed for us and our ministry: you know who you are, and I treasure you. To Greg Beckenham and your team: thank you for your life-changing ministry to us and those we minister to. To all the couples who have sat with us in our home and reached for a better relationship: thank you for increasing our joy. To our dear friends, Sam and Sanaa: thank you for the laughter, tears, and life together, for loving me, inspiring me, and encouraging me to bring what is hidden into the Light. You are mirrors of the soul.

Lastly, to my family. To my friend and soul mate, Barry: thank you for your unwavering support and encouragement, for sustaining me in ways I never knew I needed, and for sharpening me with our differences. Living with me while I'm writing is difficult, especially when I'm in another space and removed from the daily tasks of living. Thank you for cooking meals and cleaning the house when I was too preoccupied to notice. You are gifted in making the complex simple and creating structure where it is hard to find. We got through reviewing the book with our relationship still intact, whew! Thank you for blessing me by walking beside you on your journey to wholeness and wholeheartedness. It has indeed been the greatest privilege of my life.

To my son, Mark, and daughter, Rebecca: thank you for challenging me and letting me know that I gave you a path to heal from pain. You inspire me with your own journeys. I'm so proud of you and thankful to have you in my life.

# ABOUT THE AUTHOR

## Dr. Paula Davis

Dr Paula Davis is a retired clinical counsellor, supervisor, and educator specialising in psychological trauma. She has taught and supervised counselling students in university higher degree programs, both in Australia and overseas. Together with her husband, she co-authored A Safe Place: A Marriage Enrichment Resource Manual (2021) and they still deliver marriage programs internationally. Paula's books and her work is marked by cultural sensitivity, relational depth, and a compassionate commitment to healing. While she finds deep fulfilment in making a positive impact, she also treasures life's simple joys, sharing a coffee with her husband, swimming in the surf just across from her home, or exploring the outdoors. She is drawn to adventure and new experiences, from skydiving and ziplining across the Victoria Falls gorge to cage-diving with great white sharks in South Africa and walking with African lions.

# REFERENCE LIST FOR BOOK CHAPTERS

## Introduction

Thompson, F. (1983). *The Hound of Heaven*. New York: Morehouse Publishing.

## Part 1 - Wounds And The God Who Heals

### Chapter 1 - Time Does Not Heal All Wounds

Mulholland, M. R., Jr. (2006). *Invitation to a journey: A road map for spiritual formation*. InterVarsity Press.

### Chapter 2 - Tears That Open The Heart

Grace Life International. (n.d.). *Billy Graham got discouraged*. Retrieved April 15, 2025, from https://www.gracelifeinternational.com/billy-graham-got-discouraged/

Turnbull, G. (2012). *Trauma: From Lockerbie to 7/7: How trauma affects our minds and how we fight back*. London, UK: Corgi Adult Publishing.

## Chapter 3 - Wounded Love

Bible Hub. (n.d.). *2479. ischus.* Expositor's Bible Commentary. Retrieved from https://biblehub.com/greek/2479.htm

Brown, B. (2013). *The power of vulnerability - Brene Brown.* [YouTube]. Retrieved from https://youtu.be/sXSjc-pbXk4?si=1k9XypR5yx0u8kJ

Taylor, M. T. (2014). *Churning Waters.* Grey Circle Publishing.

Tennyson, A. L. (1849). *In Memoriam A.H.H.* Edward Moxon.

## Chapter 4 - My Body Remembers

Alcoholics Anonymous World Services, lnc. (2002). *Alcoholics anonymous: The story of how many thousands of men and women have recovered from alcoholism* (4th ed.). New York: Alcoholics Anonymous World Services, lnc.

Bardugo, L. (2017). *Crooked kingdom (Six of crows book 2).* London, UK: Orion Children's Books.

Davis, P. A. (2015). The broken strong. *Counselling Connections Across Australia, 6, 15-19.*

Dunbar, H. F. (1943). *Psychosomatic diagnosis.* New York: P. B. Hoeber lnc.

Dunbar, H. F. (1947). *Mind and body: Psychosomatic medicine.* New York: Random House.

Farrell, E. J. (2000). *Healing from the past: The sacrament of reconciliation.* Church Publishing.

Fisher, J. (2009). *Psychoeducational aids for working with psychological trauma - flip chart* (8th ed.). MA, USA: Center for integrative Healing.

Nouwen, H. (1979). *The wounded healer.* New York: Image, Doubleday.

Ogden, P., Minton, K., & Pain, C. (2006). Trauma and the body: A sensorimotor approach to psychotherapy. New York: W.W. Norton & Company, lnc.

Salmansohn, K. (2023). *Top 70 Karen Salmansohn Quotes.* Quotefancy. Retrieved from https://quotefancy.com/karen-salmansohn-quotes

Strong, J. (1995). *The New Strong's Exhaustive Concordance of the Bible.* Thomas Nelson.

Thayer, J. H. (1889). *Thayer's Greek-English lexicon of the New Testament.* Harper & Brothers.

## Chapter 5 - When My Thoughts Become Wounds

Iyengar, U., Kim, S., Martinez, S., Fonagy, P., & Strathearn, L. (2014). Unresolved trauma in mothers: intergenerational effects and the role of reorganization. Frontiers in Psychology, 5. Retrieved from www.frontiersin.org/journals/psychology/articles/10.3389/fpsyg.2014.00966 DOI=10.3389/fpsyg.2014.00966

Meyer, J. (1995). *Battlefield of the mind: Winning the battle in your mind.* Warner Faith.

Plutarch. (n.d.). *The Moralia* (W. C. Helmbold, Trans.). Harvard University Press.

van der Kolk, Bessel A. (1994). The Body Keeps the Score: Memory and the Evolving Psychobiology Of Post-traumatic Stress. *Harvard Review of Psychiatry*, 1,(5), 253-265. *Ovid Technologies (Wolters Kluwer Health)*, doi:10.3109/10673229409017088.

Lewis, C. S. (2023). *C. S. Lewis quotes*. Goodreads. Retrieved from: https://www.goodreads.com/quotes/13641-imagine-yourself-as-a-living-house-god-comes-in-to

## Chapter 6 - Holding Complexity In My Story

Clayton, I. (2011). *Beware of spiritual bypass: Why do we avoid rather than accept?* Psychology Today. Retrieved from https://www.psychologytoday.com/au/blog/emotional-sobriety/201110/beware-spiritual-bypass

Jones, A. (1989). *Soul making: The desert way of spirituality*. USA: HarperOne.

Tears of the sun. (2003). [Movie]. *Rotten Tomatoes*. Fandango Media. Archived from the original on September 16, 2020.

Welwood, J. (2000). *Toward a psychology of awakening: Buddhism, psychotherapy and the path of personal and spiritual transformation*. Boulder, Colorado: Shambhala Publications Inc.

## Chapter 7 - What Kept Me Stuck

Barton, R. H. (2011). *Pentecost: Celebrating the "Spirit" in spiritual transformation*. Beyond Words. https://transformingcenter.org/2011/06/what-we-believe-about-spiritual-transformation-a-biblical-and-theological-perspective/

W., Danker, F. W., Arndt, W. F., & Gingrich, F. W. (2000). *A Greek-English lexicon of the New Testament and other early Christian literature* (3rd ed.). University of Chicago Press.

Beck, A. T. (1967). *Depression: Clinical, experimental, and theoret-*

*ical aspects*. Harper & Row.

Bonaparte, N. (n.d.). *The best cure for the body is a quiet mind* [ Quote]. Attributed.

Burns, D. D. (1980). *Feeling good: The new mood therapy*. William Morrow and Company.

De Silva, D. (2017). *Shifting atmospheres: A strategy for victorious spiritual warfare*. Destiny Image Publishers.

Ellis, A. (2004). *Rational emotive behavior therapy: It works for me —It can work for you*. Amherst, NY: Prometheus Books.

Harper, D. (n.d.). *Worry*. In *Online Etymology Dictionary*. Retrieved April 15, 2025, from https://www.etymonline.com/word/worry

Henigsberg, N., Kalember, P., Petrović, Z. K., & Šečić, A. (2019). Neuroimaging research in posttraumatic stress disorder – Focus on amygdala, hippocampus and prefrontal cortex. *Progress in Neuropsychopharmacology & Biological Psychiatry, 90*, 37–42. https://doi.org/10.1016/j.pnpbp.2018.11.003

Neria, Y., Solomon, Z., & Dekel, R. (2024). Neuroimaging of posttraumatic stress disorder in adults and youth. *Molecular Psychiatry*. https://doi.org/10.1038/s41380-024-02558-w

Nock, A. J. (1928). *The Theory of Education in the United States*. Harcourt, Brace and Company.

Vivyan, C. (2009). *Mental crusher.* Retrieved from https://www.getselfhelp.co.uk/docs/MentalCrusher.pdf

## Chapter 8 - Healing My Soul Wounds

Eldredge, J. (n.d.). *One Minute Pause* [Mobile application

software]. Wild at Heart. Retrieved April 15, 2025, from https://wildatheart.org/apps/one-minute-pause

Frost, J. (2006). *Experiencing Fathers embrace*. PA, USA: Destiny Image Publishers.

Moore, T. (2016). *Care of the soul: A guide for cultivating depth and sacredness in everyday life* (25th anniversary ed.). USA: HarperCollins.

Rumi. (1995). *The Essential Rumi* (C. Barks, Trans.). HarperOne.

St. Augustine. (1991). *Confessions* (H. Chadwick, Trans.). Oxford University Press. *(Original work written ca. 397–400 CE)*

Weil, S. (1942b). The Love of God and Affliction. In Panichas, G. A. (1977). *The Simone Weil Reader*. New York: David McKay Co.

Weil, S. (1943a). Human Personality. In Miles, S. (1986). *Simone Weil: An Anthology*. New York: Grove Press.

Weil, S. (1973). *Waiting for God* (1st ed.). New York: Harper & Row.

## Chapter 9 - My Soul Laid Bare

Brown, F., Driver, S. R., & Briggs, C. A. (2000). *The Brown-Driver-Briggs Hebrew-English Lexicon*. Hendrickson Publishers.

Poindexter, C. (2013, May 14). *And in the end, we were all just humans... drunk on the idea that love, only love, could heal our brokenness* [Tweet]. Twitter. https://twitter.com/healthesebones/status/334591331968655360

Strong, J. (1995). *The exhaustive concordance of the Bible: Showing every word of the text of the common English version and every occurrence of each word in regular order* (electronic ed.). Hendrickson Publishers.

## Chapter 10 - When The Spirit Shatters


Akashi, Y. J., Nef, H. M., & Lyon, A. R. (2015). Epidemiology and pathophysiology of Takotsubo syndrome. *Nature Reviews Cardiology, 12*(7), 387–397. https://doi.org/10.1038/nrcardio.2015.38

Fahkry, T. (2017). *Why your emotional wounds strengthen you.* Mission.org. Retrieved from https://medium.com/the-mission/why-your-emotional-wounds-strengthen-you-4b5dff0cae20

Frey, W.H. (1985). *Crying: The mystery of tears.* Minneapolis: Winston Press.

Neufeld, G. (2010). *Transformative parenting workshop.* CA, USA:

Nelson, J. K. (2009). An attachment perspective on crying in psychotherapy. In J. H. Obegi & E. Berant (Eds.), *Attachment theory and research in clinical work with adults* (pp. 328-347). New York, NY, US: Guilford Press.

Strong, J. (1995). *The exhaustive concordance of the Bible: Showing every word of the text of the common English version and every occurrence of each word in regular order* (electronic ed.). Hendrickson Publishers.

Wiseman, E. (2022). 'Clinically awful': why the pain of a broken heart is real. *The Guardian.* Retrieved from https://www.theguardian.com/lifeandstyle/2022/aug/28/clinically-awful-why-the-pain-of-a-broken-heart-is-real

Williams, F. (2022). Op-Ed: Heartbreak hurts, in part because our cells 'listen for loneliness'. Los Angeles Times. Retrieved from https://www.latimes.com/opinion/story/2022-02-06/loneliness-white-blood-cells-inflammation-chronic-disease-neurogenomics

## Chapter 11 - When God Was Used Against Me

Alder, S. L. (n.d.). Spiritual Abuse Quotes. Goodreads. Retrieved from https://www.goodreads.com/quotes/tag/spiritual-abuse

Callahan II, R. G. (2024). *Fire in the whole: Embracing our righteous anger with white Christianity and reclaiming our wholeness.* UK: Westminster John Knox Press.

Jones, A. (1989). *Soul making: The desert way of spirituality.* USA: HarperOne.

Sinason, V. (n.d.). Spiritual Abuse Quotes. Goodreads. Retrieved from https://www.goodreads.com/quotes/tag/spiritual-abuse

Tears of the sun. (2003). [Movie]. *Rotten Tomatoes.* Fandango Media. Archived from the original on September 16, 2020.

Weil, S. (1943a). Human Personality. In Miles, S. (1986). *Simone Weil: An Anthology.* New York: Grove Press.

Welwood, J. (2000). Toward a psychology of awakening: Buddhism, psychotherapy and the path of personal and spiritual transformation. Boulder, Colorado: Shambhala Publications Inc.

## Part 2 - The War Within: Shame And Identity

## Chapter 12 - The Devil's Pact: Lies I Agree To

Bradshaw, J. (2005). *Healing the shame that binds you.* USA: Health Communications.

Brown, B. (2012). *Daring greatly: How the courage to be vulnerable transforms the way we live, love, parent, and lead* (1st ed). USA: Avery.

Brown, B., & Hartling, L. (2016). *Shame shields: The armor we use to protect ourselves and why it doesn't serve us.* Retrieved from: https://catalog.psychotherapy.com.au/sq/pz_001195_brenebrown_email-32850

Clinton, T., & Sibcy, G. (2006). *Why you do the things you do: The secret to healthy relationships.* Nashville, TN: Thomas Nelson.

Earle, D. W. (2014). *Love is not enough: Changing dysfunctional family habits.* CreateSpace Independent Publishing Platform.

Heitzmann, K. (2004). *Secrets* (Michelli Family Series #1). Bethany House Publishers.

Horney, K. (1950). *Neurosis and human growth: The struggle toward self-realization.* New York, NY: W. W. Norton & Company.

Nouwen, H. J. M. (2002). *Life of the Beloved: Spiritual living in a secular world.* NY: Crossroad Publishing.

Rohr, R. (1987). *Broken and blessed: A retreat.* Retrieved from http://link.bu.edu/portal/Broken-and-blessed--a-retreat-Richard-Rohr./D_V-h-I4-Hw/

Rohr, R. (2013). *The sacred wound: Meditation 22 of 53: Richard Rohr's daily meditation.* Retrieved from https://myemail.constantcontact.com/Richard-Rohr-s-Daily-Meditation----August-17--2013.html?soid=1103098668616&aid=VsvGk1wUnuI

Townsend, J. (1996). Hiding from love: How to change the withdrawal patterns that isolate and imprison you. USA:

Zondervan.

Walker, A. (1990). *The temple of my familiar.* New York, Pocket.

## Chapter 13 - The God I Couldn't Trust

Allender, D. B. (2014). *The wounded heart: Healing for adult victims of child sexual abuse.* USA: The Navigators.

Arrupe, P. (2004). *Pedro Arrupe: Essential Writings* (K. Burke, Ed.). Orbis Books.

Birch, J. (n.d.). *Faith and worship.* Worship, Prayers & Bible Study resources. Retrieved from https://www.faithandworship.com/#gsc.tab=0

Hybels, B. (n.d.). *Five dangerous ways of praying.* Retrieved from https://www.rsfgc.org/five_dangerous_prayers.htm

Tozer, A. W. (2017). *The knowledge of the Holy*. CA, USA: Fig Publishing.

Voskamp, A. (n.d.). Meet Ann. Retrieved from https://annvoskamp.com/ann-voskamp/

## Chapter 14 - Is God Truly Good? My Wrestling With His Character

Markova, D. (2000). *I will not die an unlived life: Reclaiming purpose and passion*. Conari Press.

Merriam-Webster. (n.d.). *Surrender*. In *Merriam-Webster.com dictionary*. Retrieved April 16, 2025, from https://www.merriam-webster.com/dictionary/surrender

Nelson, A. E. (2002). *Embracing brokenness: How God refines us through life's disappointments.* CO, USA: Navpress.

Pascal, B. (2004). *Pensées* (W. F. Trotter, Trans.). Dover Publications. (Original work published 1670)Voskamp. https://annvoskamp.com/2022/10/5-secrets-to-an-awesome-life-even-in-the-midst-of-some-awful-traumatic-days/

Rohr, R. (2009). *The naked now: Learning to see as the mystics see*. Crossroad Publishing Company.

Strong, J. (1890). *Strong's exhaustive concordance of the Bible*. Abingdon Press. (Hebrew word H7291, *radaph*)

Voskamp, A. (2022, October 14). *5 secrets to an awesome life (even in the midst of some awful traumatic days).*

Walsch, N. D. (1995). *Conversations with God, Book 1: An uncommon dialogue*. Putnam.

## Chapter 15 - The Faces Of Shame

Allender, D. B., & Longman, T. III. (1994). *The Cry of the Soul: How Our Emotions Reveal Our Deepest Questions About God.* NavPress.

Brown, B. (2012, June). *Listening to shame* [Video]. TED. https://www.ted.com/talks/brene_brown_listening_to_shame

Budden, A. (2009). The role of shame in posttraumatic stress disorder: A proposal for a socio emotional model for DSM-V. Science and Medicine, 69(7), 1032-1039. http://dx.doi.org/10.1016/j.socscimed.2009.07.032

Cloud, H., & Townsend, J. (2017). *Boundaries: When to say yes, how to say no to take control of your life* (Updated and expanded ed.). Zondervan.

Fossum, M. A., & Mason, M. J. (1989). *Facing shame: Families in recovery.* New York: W. W. Norton & Company.

Herman, J. L. (2006). *Trauma and recovery: The aftermath of violence – From domestic abuse to political terror* (Lithuanian ed.). Vaga.

Kaufman, G. (2004). *The psychology of shame: Theory and treatment of shame-based syndromes* (2nd ed.). USA: Springer Publishing Company.

Nouwen, H. (2002). *Life of the Beloved.* New York: Crossroads.

Schore, A. N. (1994). *Affect regulation and the origin of the self: The neurobiology of emotional development.* Mahweh, New Jersey: Erlbaum.

Seamands, D. A. (1981). *Healing for damaged emotions.* Victor Books.

## Chapter 16 - The Self I Rejected

Brown, B. (2004). *An interview with Brené Brown, Ph.D.* The Mothers Movement Online. Retrieved from http://www.mothersmovement.org/features/bbrown_int/bbrown_int_3.htm

Brown, B. (2008). *I thought it was just me (but it isn't): Telling the truth about perfectionism, inadequacy, and power.* USA: Gotham Books.

Brown, B. (2015). *Rising strong: The reckoning, the rumble, the revolution.* Spiegel & Grau.

Clinton, T. & Sibcy, G. (2002). Attachments: Why you love, feel, and act the way you do. USA: Thomas Nelson Publishers.

Cozolino, L. (2013). *The social neuroscience of education: Optimizing attachment and learning in the classroom.* New York: W.W. Norton & Co.

Gilligan, J. (2016). *Violence: The enduring problem* (3rd ed.). USA:

SAGE Publications, Inc.

Hughes, D. A. (2010). *Facilitating developmental attachment: The road to emotional recovery and behavioural change in foster and adopted children.* USA: Jason Aronson Inc. Publishers.

Nouwen, H. J. M. (2013). *A cry for mercy: Prayers from the Genesee.* New York, NY: Images Publishing.

Stern, D. (2000). *The interpersonal world of the infant: A view from psychoanalysis and developmental psychology.* New York: Basic Books.

Teyber, E. (2005). *Interpersonal process in psychotherapy: A relational approach* (4th ed.). Australia: Brooks/Cole.

Townsend, J. (2001). *Hiding from love: How to change the withdrawal patterns that isolate and imprison you.* Zondervan.

## Chapter 17 - Unpacking The Weight Of Shame

Brown, B. (2007). *I thought it was just me (but it isn't): Making the journey from "What will people think?" to "I am enough".* Gotham Books.

Brown, B. (2012). *Daring greatly: How the courage to be vulnerable transforms the way we live, love, parent, and lead.* Gotham Books.

Brown, B. (2015). *Rising strong: The reckoning, the rumble, the revolution.* Spiegel & Grau.

Calhoun, A. (2005). *Spiritual disciplines handbook: Practices that transform us.* Downers Grove, IL: Intervarsity Press.

Emerson, R. W. (n.d.). *24 killer quotes about identity to find your true self.* Flâneur Life. Retrieved from https://www.flaneurlife.com/quotes-about-identity/

Kelman, S. G. (Ed.). (2009). The social contract: Summary. *Masterpieces of World Literature, Critical Edition.* eNotes.com, Inc. Retrieved from http://www

Nin, A. (n.d.). *Shame is the lie someone told you about yourself.*

Rich, A., Gelphi, B. C., & Gelphi, A. (1993). *Adrienne Rich's poetry and prose.* New York: Norton & Co.

Seamands, D. (2015). *Healing for damaged emotions.* CO, USA: David C. Cook.

Uchino, B. N., Cacioppo, J. T., & Kiecolt-Glaser, J. K. (1996). The relationship between social support and physiological processes: A review with emphasis on underlying mechanisms and implications for health. *Psychological Bulletin, 119*(3), 488–531. https://doi.org/10.1037/0033-2909.119.3.488

West, M. (2012). *Hello, My Name Is* [Song]. On *Into the Light.* Sparrow Records.

## Chapter 18 - Rewriting Shame

Alder, S. L. (n.d.). Judas quotes. Goodreads. Retreived from https://www.goodreads.com/quotes/tag/judas?page=2

Ayivor, I. (n.d.). Judas quotes. Goodreads. Retreived from https://www.goodreads.com/quotes/tag/judas?page=2

Card, O. S. (2001). *Shadow of the Hegemon.* Tor Books.

Green, T. (2007). *When the well runs dry: Prayer beyond the beginnings.* USA: Ave Maria Press.

www.ingramcontent.com/pod-product-compliance
Lightning Source LLC
LaVergne TN
LVHW050617100826
845148LV00011B/1625

* 9 7 8 0 6 4 5 1 1 7 9 5 0 *